Z88
COMPUTING

Z88
COMPUTING

IAN SINCLAIR

David Fulton Publishers

London

David Fulton Publishers Ltd
14 Chalton Drive London N2 0QW

First published in Great Britain by
David Fulton Publishers 1988

Reprinted April 1988

Copyright©Ian Sinclair 1988

British Library Cataloguing in Publication Data

Sinclair, Ian R.
 Z88 Computing
 1. Cambridge Z88 (Computer System)
 2. Computable functions—Data processing
 I. Title
 004.1′25   QA9.39

ISBN 1-85346-045-1

Typeset by Chapterhouse, Formby
Printed and bound in Great Britain by
Biddles Ltd., Guildford

Contents

Contents

Preface

The Z88 is a genuine lap-top computer which incorporates a considerable amount of useful business software within its deceptively slim outline. Small, however, does not imply simple, and users whose main experience of computers has been with the PC type of machine may not find it easy to come to grips with the differences that are inherent in the Z88 approach. In particular, since the basic machine has no disk system and relies entirely on electronic memory, the user must quickly get used to the methods of transferring data to another machine (usually a PC) or to printing data on to paper. These methods are not dealt with in the manual.

Since the machine uses its own built-in programs, with no provision for making use of the standard office type of programs such as WordStar, SuperCalc or dBASE-3, a thorough understanding of how the effects of word-processing, spreadsheet use and database action are achieved with the built-in programs is important. The outstanding virtue of the machine is that it allows the production of a document that contains text, spreadsheet data and database data all together. In addition, this can be done anywhere, in a hotel room, in a train, in the passenger seat of a car – the only requirement is sufficient illumination so that the screen in visible.

This book is not intended to replace the manual, which is the ultimate reference source, but to guide the user so that you can get the best from the machine as quickly as possible. As with all computers, some knowledge of programming is needed in order to unlock actions (like programmable calculations) that the more advanced user might require, but this type of action is not dealt with here. The advanced filing system commands, and the topic of command line interpreter (CLI) files have also been omitted since many users will find no need for them, and only the experienced and skilled user will be able to use them to advantage.

The book has been organised so that it can be used in two ways. One is as a progressive familiarisation course in the machine, starting with the simplest actions and progressing to the use of the

PipeDream program. The other is as a reference book, allowing you to look up compact descriptions of how effects can be achieved.

The examples shown in this book have been printed on an Epson RX-80 dot matrix printer fitted with a serial interface. The serial cable I used was converted from one used for a QL computer, but obviously a Z88 serial cable will be available by the time this book appears. Since this book deals with the Z88 as an ancillary to a PC type of machine, the transfer of data between machines is also covered. For owners of the Amstrad PC1512/1640 machines a method of transfer is detailed which requires no special software and can be carried out with a simple adaptor lead connected to the serial cable. For Amstrad owners, this could represent a consider-able saving in costs, and the method is adaptable for other computers. In the course of writing this book, files were regularly transferred between an Amstrad PC and the Z88, allowing me to work with the unexpanded machine throughout.

I am, as always, very grateful to many people whose efforts have combined to produce this book. My special thanks must go to David Fulton, who provided both the computer (bought over the counter from Dixons) and the proposal, and to the editing staff who laboured to convert my disk into a real book.

Ian Sinclair, Autumn 1987

Part 1
Introduction

Since the aim of this book is to allow you to become familiar with the use of the Z88, the order of items is very different from that used in the manual. The simpler popdown type of programs are dealt with first, followed by the Diary and then by the very much more complex PipeDream.

This allows topics such as cursor movement to be dealt with by simple examples, and avoids having to plunge into advanced work simply to illustrate an action.

The relative amount of space devoted to topics should not be taken as any indication of their relative importance. Two Parts have been devoted to the word-processing actions of PipeDream because the full range of commands can be demonstrated with text, and these commands do not then have to be explained again when the use of PipeDream for spreadsheets is being illustrated. Because of this, you should not assume that you can omit the topic of word-processing because your primary interest is in the use of spreadsheets or databases. The Database part of this book is very brief because so many of the actions have been covered in previous parts.

Setting up

The machine should be prepared for use as described in the manual, pages 6–9. Note the following points:

1 Use the mains adaptor rather than the batteries if you are working near a mains point.

2 Never unclip the battery cover while you are working with the machine (you might inadvertently do this while unfolding the stand). Disturbing the batteries can cause a loss of power which can sometimes require the machine to be reset, losing stored work.

3 Remember that the memory size of the machine is very limited in its basic state (with no added memory). You should therefore aim to transfer or print stored material as soon as possible.

4 The machine is never truly switched off. When you press both SHIFT keys to 'switch off', only the screen display and the keyboard entry are disabled. The memory circuits are still switched on in order to store your data.

5 Never change the batteries unless you have the machine working on the mains adaptor. There is an internal emergency supply (a capacitor) which will keep the memory working for a few minutes when batteries and mains supply are both withdrawn, but you should never rely on this if your computer contains vital data.

6 You should memorise as soon as possible the procedure for deleting suspended work. This is because when the memory fills up, only the abbreviated commands will be accepted. (See Section 6.)

■ SECTION 2

The built-in software

The Z88 contains two types of built-in software programs, in the form of applications and the popdowns. An application program will run when started with a command (using the key marked with the square symbol), and is suspended in the memory when you start to use another program.

You can return to a suspended application program later by requesting it from a list of choices marked SUSPENDED ACTIVITIES. This is done by moving the shaded cursor bar over the title of the suspended program and pressing ENTER.

A popdown is an item that you can consult (like a calendar) while working with a program and which is not left suspended in memory when you are finished with it. The popdown can be made to pop up again out of the way when you have finished with it.

The applications programs of the Z88 are PipeDream, Diary, BASIC, Terminal, and PrinterEd. Not all of these are of equal importance, and this book will not cover the use of BASIC, which is a programming language with which you can create your own applications. Terminal and PrinterEd require rather more knowledge of the machine that you will have in the initial stages.

The popdowns are Index, Calculator, Calendar, Clock, Alarm, Filer, Panel and Import/Export. Of these, Index is the most frequently used, Panel probably least, and Import/Export, though more complicated, is necessary for transferring data to other computers, in particular to a PC type of machine.

1 PipeDream is a large and complicated program which combines the actions of work-processing, spreadsheet preparation and use, and database applications.

2 Diary is used, as the name suggests, to keep the equivalent of an appointments diary. It can be used in conjunction with the Calendar popdown. Unlike a diary kept on paper, the contents of this Diary can be searched for names.

3 Terminal is used in transferring data between machines, and requires some knowledge of computing.

4   PrinterEd is a program for determining how a printer will deal with data from the Z88. If you are using an Epson printer or a printer that is described as being Epson-compatible, then you will not need PrinterEd except to add a few refinements (see Part 9).

5   The Index popdown is used to gain access to all of the applications programs and popdowns. It also allows you to check for the presence of memory cards that you may have added to the basic machine.

6   The Calculator is a simple type of calculator which incorporates most features of a pocket calculator but is slightly more bother to use. It includes some very useful unit conversions, however, such as gallons to litres.

7   The Clock, Calendar and Alarm provide timing and reminders for you. The alarm can provide an audible warning as well as indicating on the screen what is to be done.

8   The Filer allows you to store data in the memory (in the future, possibly to a disk) rather than holding the data as a suspended activity. In this book, we shall deal only with the simpler aspects of using the Filer in conjunction with other programs.

9   The Panel allows you to choose for yourself the way that various actions work, such as how soon a key action will repeat when you hold the key down, whether you get a sound on pressing a key, whether pressing a key inserts a character or overprints a character.

10   Import/Export provides a set of four simple commands for transferring data between computers. If you are transferring between two Z88 machines, nothing more is needed, but if you are transferring between the Z88 and a PC machine you may need suitable software for the PC machine. Part 9 describes how transfers may be made to and from the Amstrad PC machines with no extra software.

■ SECTION 3

The cursor keys

The cursor keys are marked with arrows and located on the right-hand bottom corner of the keyboard. The action of these keys can also be modified by pressing other keys at the same time. The actions are used in both PipeDream and Diary.

1 Using the right or left cursor keys will move the flashing cursor by one character right or left. Using the up or down cursor keys will move the cursor by one line up or down.

2 Using SHIFT along with a cursor key gives a greater range of movement. SHIFT with left or right moves by one word, SHIFT with up or down moves one screen amount, eight lines.

3 Using the diamond key along with the cursor keys gives a further range of movement. Diamond with left or right moves to the start or finish of a line, diamond with up or down moves to top or bottom of that vertical column.

4 The square keys along with left or right allows you to move the margins of a document by one character in the selected direction.

5 The TAB key will move the cursor from one lettered column to the next on the right. If you have not altered the settings on the machine, this corresponds to a distance of twelve characters. Using SHIFT TAB will cause the cursor to move left.

■ SECTION 4

Diamond and square keys

The keys that are marked with the diamond (between SHIFT and TAB) and the square (left of spacebar) are used extensively for commands. You are not forced to make use of these keys, because the Index and Menu system of the Z88 can be used for all of your choices.

One important difference, however, is speed of use. When you make use of the Index and Menu system, you have to wait for details to be printed on the screen, select the item you want by moving the cursor, and then press the ENTER key. This takes time, not least because it takes some time for the screen to change. If you know the 'shorthand' code for the action you want, then pressing a few keys (very often only two) will achieve your purpose more quickly.

In addition, if you have nearly filled the memory, you can no longer use the screen system for commands. You can still issue commands with the keycodes (diamond or square plus letter key), however.

1 The key marked with the square is used in calling up applications and popdowns. In the following list, the square symbol is represented as □ :

- □ A **Alarm**
- □ B **BASIC**
- □ C **Calendar**
- □ D **Diary**
- □ E **PrinterEd**
- □ F **Filer**
- □ P **PipeDream**
- □ R **Calculator**
- □ S **Panel**
- □ T **Clock**
- □ V **Terminal**
- □ X **Import/Export**

Several of these are easy to remember because of the use of letters in the applications/popdown names. Others can be remembered with some effort, such as using □ T for Time (Clock) or □ X for Import/Export. The least memorable, □ V for Terminal is also the least-needed in the context of this book.

The square key is also used with a few other keys (the cursor left and right, for example) for other purposes. We shall deal with these as we come to them.

2 The key marked with the diamond shape is used in selecting actions within applications or popdowns. The most common of these are marked on the casing of the machine immediately below the screen. A full list is given in Appendix A.

3 These square and diamond keys can be used in either of two ways. You can hold the key down while you type the letter keys that follow, or you can simply press the keys in sequence. When you press the square or the diamond key, you will see the symbol appear on the right-hand edge of the screen, and if the command that follows uses more than one letter, you will see the letters also.

■ SECTION 5
The ENTER and ESC keys

The ENTER key on the Z88 corresponds to the key that on other computers is marked ENTER, RETURN, or with the symbol of the return arrow (down and left).

1 When you are working with menu items, pressing the ENTER key will carry out the action described in the line on which the cursor is resting (usually also marked by a shaded bar).

2 When you are entering text in PipeDream, Diary or other applications that will accept text, pressing ENTER creates a new paragraph, forcing a new line to be taken.

3 You do not need to press ENTER when you get near the end of a line on the screen if you have more to type. Unlike a typewriter, a computer allows word-wrap, meaning that your typing will automatically be continued on the next line without splitting a word.

4 You will probably use ENTER more often when you are entering data into a spreadsheet or database, when it has the meaning of 'enter data into machine'.

5 The ESC key is used to move from your present task (using an application or a popdown) to the *previous* one. You can remember this by referring to this key as the ESCape key.

6 A few applications do not use the ESC key in this way. You can escape from Terminal, for example, by using SHIFT ENTER, but you can, in any case, leave any application or popdown by pressing the INDEX key. This will be needed if you leave Diary or PipeDream with data that has not been stored elsewhere (in RAM, for example).

7 Leaving an application program with the INDEX key will cause the application to be suspended, so that you can return to it even if you have created another document.

The uncanny silence of the rubbery keys can be converted to a slight bleep – more like a click – by using a popdown option. If you press INDEX and select PANEL you will see that using the down-cursor key will get you to the line marked Keyclick No.

With the cursor on this line, pressing the Y key will convert this to yes, and give you a keyclick from then on. You can then leave PANEL by pressing ESC. The effect can be cancelled by selecting PANEL again and pressing N on the keyclick line.

INDEX and MENU

The terms INDEX and MENU can be confusing, particularly if you have encountered them used in other ways on other computers.

1 The INDEX is the master list of applications and popdowns. You select what you want to do from this list or by using the square key commands of this list.

2 When you are using an application or a popdown, you can always jump to another by using the INDEX key. Any pop-down that you have been using will be abandoned. If you have jumped from an application by using the INDEX, that application becomes suspended and will be held in memory just as you left it.

3 If you suspend too many activities, the memory will become filled, and you will no longer be able to select from the INDEX menu except by using the square key commands. When this happens, you must KILL some of the suspended activities. You might need to save some data before you do this – be careful.

4 To KILL a suspended activity, look at the list of suspended activities that is shown along with the INDEX list (press INDEX to get this list if you have not already done so). Move the cursor bar to an action you want to delete, and then press the diamond key and type KILL (capitals or lower-case letters are equally acceptable). The screen will blank for a moment, and the suspended activity will be removed.

5 The MENU key is used to find the range of actions that can be employed from within an application or a popdown. To make use of the menu key, you must have something from the INDEX menu running.

6 Pressing the MENU key will produce a list of choices on the left-hand side of the screen, with one in bold print. The bold-print item is the main heading for a set of actions, and pressing ENTER will list these items. Figure 1.1 illustrates the MENU choices in the various programs – note that some programs have no MENU items.

7 You can then use the list on the screen as advice or as commands. The commands can be executed by moving the cursor over the command and pressing ENTER, or by using the code shown which will usually be a diamond key and letter code.

8 To get back to the main program, press ESC. To get to another set of menu items, press the MENU key again. Note that you cannot use the cursor keys on the main MENU list, you can only move down the list by pressing the MENU key until the items repeat.

Program from INDEX	MENU choice items				
PipeDream	Blocks	Cursor	Edit	Files	Layout
	Options	Print			
Diary	Blocks	Cursor	Edit	Files	
INDEX	Commands				
Filer	Commands				
PrinterEd	Cursor	Files			
Panel	Cursor	Files			
Terminal	Commands				

Figure 1.1 The MENU choices that exist in different programs.

■ SECTION 7

Using memory

All data is stored in the memory of the basic Z88 machine. This memory is arranged into sections, however, so that when you are told that the memory is full of suspended applications this does not mean that you have to lose valuable data. Figure 1.2 describes the additional memory provisions.

Memory Expansion

The Z88 is expanded by plugging memory cartridges into the three numbered rectangular receptacles at the front. The cartridges that you can plug in can consist of either:

(a)   Additional memory that you can use for storing files, or
(b)   New programs in cartridge form.

The types of additional memory cartridge are described as RAM or EPROM. The RAM cartridges act like an extension of the type of memory that is already fitted for your use. The EPROM cartridges can have data 'burned in', making this data almost permanent. If you remove a RAM cartridge, the data on it will be lost, but when an EPROM cartridge is removed, this has no effect on the stored data.

These cartridges come in three sizes, 32K, 128K and 1M. The 32K cartridge has space for 32768 characters, the 128K for 131072 characters (K means 1024). This compares with the absolute maximum of about 14K which is available to you in the unexpanded machine. The 1M cartridge allows 1024K characters.

Figure 1.2   Provision for extending the memory.

1 When you find that you cannot use any more suspended activities, you have the choice to KILL a file, as detailed in Section 6.4. If all of your files are important, you can save one or more to another part of the memory that is used for filing.

2 To save a PipeDream file, select the file name on the suspended list by moving the shaded bar over the name with the cursor keys. Press ENTER to gain access to the data, and then press the diamond key, followed by FS. You will be asked for a name, and you can use up to twelve letters (more on this subject follows in other Parts). Press ENTER to save the file. You now have to delete the suspended part by using KILL. A Diary file is saved in a similar way.

3 Though you can find how much memory is left available for a current PipeDream (diamond O) or Diary (diamond EMF) document, you cannot find in any simple way how much memory is available for files. You should therefore transfer files to another machine or print them out as soon as possible after creating them.

4 Remember that each time you enter an application like PipeDream, you are starting a new document and a previous one will be suspended. If you want to continue with a previous document, you need to select this from the INDEX list.

Part 2
The Popdowns

Clock, Calendar, Alarm and Calculator

In this Part we shall deal with four popdown programs that are extensively used both in their own right and as items to consult during the use of the main applications programs. The clock and the calendar are linked in the sense that setting the clock also corrects the date setting for the calendar.

The calendar is linked to the Diary program (Part 3) because it controls the day for which diary entry or reading is done. The clock and calendar are also linked to the Alarm setting in the sense that incorrect clock or calendar setting will result in incorrect Alarm operation.

The calculator is intended for casual use while preparing documents, and would not be a serious replacement for a pocket calculator for any other purpose. The other Popdowns, and some applications programs, are used less often and always in conjunction with other programs, so that they will be dealt as and when needed. The first of the Popdowns for our purpose is the clock.

NOTE: From here on, the square and diamond keys will be shown as □ and ◇ respectively.

■ SECTION 8

The Clock display

1 Press ☐ T (square and T keys). The easiest way to remember the letter key is T for Time. The clock display will appear about ⅔rds of the way across the screen.

2 When the clock is first used, both time and date will have to be set. The time will thereafter have to be reset only for summer time changes unless there have been problems with a battery change.

3 When the Clock popdown appears, the cursor is over EXIT, meaning that pressing ESC or ENTER will return you to normal working. To set the Clock, move the cursor to SET, using either left or right cursor key. The display will appear as in Fig. 2.1.

CLOCK

Friday
25th September
1987

08:46:22

EXIT   SET

Figure 2.1 The clock display, obtained using ☐ T.

4 When you select SET, you are first asked to set the date, which is shown in the form DD/MM/19YY. If the date is incorrect, as it may be when the computer is new, you can type the day (01, 12, 20 for example), month number and year. You are not forced to enter zeros – dates such as 2/7/88 are perfectly acceptable – but you may have to use the SHIFT and DEL keys to remove an unwanted portion of an old date unless you keep to two digits for day and month and four for year.

5 Note that you are not confined to the current date, and if you want to work with a calendar for 1815 you can type this year rather than the current one. You do not need to type each digit if some are correct, and when you type you will replace the digit on which the small cursor rests. Do not remove the slash signs (/) when you type the date, and replace them if you erase them inadvertently.

6 After typing the date, or if you do not want to change the date press the down cursor key to move the cursor to the time display. Type the time in hours and minutes (in the form 09:43 for example, though 9:5:0 is acceptable if you delete any left-over digits), using the 24-hour format. Note that you must use the 24-hour format for altering the time, and the display will be in this same form, whatever the manual states. After initial setting, you will normally need to change only one digit of the hour number. Do not remove the colons (:) from the time display.

7 The time that you have typed remains frozen (it is not updated) untill you press ENTER. For that reason, when you are setting the clock time it's best to type a time a minute or so in the future, setting the seconds to 00, such as 10:04:00, and press ENTER on a time signal (TIM, digital clock, or Teletext time display) to synchronise the clock.

8 After you have pressed ENTER, the clock starts timing, and the cursor moves the EXIT, so that you can leave the clock display by using ESC or ENTER.

9 Note that once the clock is set dates are displayed in full e.g. Tuesday 8th September 1987 and the clock shows time in 24-hour form, not the AM/PM form illustrated in the manual. The list of suspended activities that is obtained from the INDEX will also show Today and Yesterday, using dates only for more remote periods.

■ SECTION 9

The Calendar

The Calendar, like the Clock, will pop down on top of any applications program. The keys that are needed to produce the Calendar are ☐ C, and when the Calendar for the current month appears, the current date is marked with a cursor.

The correct date is set from the Clock popdown which should be corrected as detailed in Section 8. It is most unlikely that you will need to set the date again unless you are crossing time zones or have allowed the batteries to run completely down. You can, however, reset the date in order to produce a calendar for some year in the distant past or future.

1 The Calendar display always shows the current month if the date has been correctly set. To change the day on which the cursor rests, use the cursor left/right and up/down keys. These keys have *wrap-around* action, meaning that if you try to move the cursor off one edge of the calendar display, it will be moved to the opposite edge instead.

2 To change the month, press the SHIFT key along with the cursor up key to obtain the calendar for the previous month, or SHIFT with the cursor down key to get the following month.

3 If you press the ◇ (diamond key) along with the up-cursor key, the calendar month (and day) will remain unchanged, but the year alters to the previous year. Using ◇ and the down-cursor key changes the year to the following year. Figure 2.2 is a reminder of calendar-hopping.

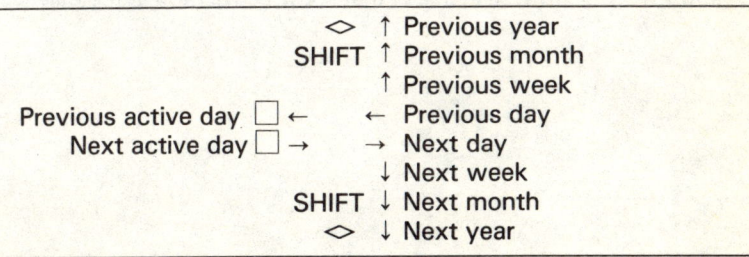

	◇ ↑ Previous year
	SHIFT ↑ Previous month
	↑ Previous week
Previous active day ☐ ←	← Previous day
Next active day ☐ →	→ Next day
	↓ Next week
	SHIFT ↓ Next month
	◇ ↓ Next year

Figure 2.2 How to move about the Calendar.

4 You can also request a calendar display for any year. With the Calendar displayed, press ENTER. The words *Look for:* will appear under the main display, and a flashing cursor will be placed over the first digit of the current calendar date. You can now type in a date such as 16/08/1947 (you need not type the 19 part of the year or the zero part of the month) and press ENTER to get the calendar for this month and year, with the cursor over the requested date. This is very useful to find on what day any date occurred.

5 The Calendar operates back to 1753 for the benefit of historians, and forwards to 9999 for optimists and writers of science fiction.

6 To leave the Calendar, press ESC. This will return you to whatever activity was in progress before the Calendar was called.

7 The Calendar has an additional action when it is called from the Diary (see Part 3). When the ☐ C keys are used to popdown the Calendar, some days will be marked with an arrowhead, as in Fig. 2.3. These are days for which there is a Diary entry (active days). By moving the cursor to such a day before pressing ESC, the diary for that day can be consulted.

JANUARY 1988

MON	TUE	WED	THU	FRI	SAT	SUN
				1	2 Today	3
4	Active ►5	6	7	8	9	10
11	days 12	Active 13	14	15	16	17
18	19	►20	21	22	23	24
25	26	days 27	28	29	30	31

Figure 2.3 The arrowhead marks that show active days in the Calendar.

■ SECTION 10

The Alarm

As the name suggests, the Alarm can be used to sound a warning and make a message appear. The sound is very faint, but it can be used whether the Z88 is switched on or off. If you have set the alarm for a time when you will be using the Z88, you can opt to turn the sound off, and rely on the message along with a bell symbol flashing under the OZ letters at the right-hand side of the screen.

If the Z88 is likely to be switched off when the Alarm time is reached (remember that the machine will switch itself off after a short time if no keys have been pressed), then when the alarm sounds, the machine is locked out. This means that though the machine appears to be switched on and working, most of the keys have no effect. To regain control switch off (both SHIFT keys) and then on again.

You can put a phrase or a command into the Alarm setting. The phrase will be printed on screen when the Alarm time is due, and if you have used a command then an operation, like running an application (Diary or PipeDream, for example) will start or resume.

The Alarm system also allows for repeated alarms which will recur at specified intervals (one second to several years) for as many times as you like (from once to 65535 times).

1 Call up the Alarm by pressing ☐ A. The two options that you can choose are EXIT or SET if the Alarm is not already set. The display will show the current date and time, with the cursor placed over the first digit of the date. You can now type a new date and/or time in the same way as you set the Clock. Remember that times are typed in 24-hour format.

2 You can also add a message of up to twenty-two characters. This message will appear on the screen if you have been using PipeDream or Diary when the Alarm sounded, but if you have been using INDEX or other non-text program, you will receive the message only by switching to Alarm (press ☐ A).

3 If the alarm is sounded with the machine off, the message does not appear automatically. The bleeper sounds (unless you have switched it off), and the bell symbol appears at the right-hand side of the screen, with the words LOCK OUT replacing the normal OZ. This should remind you to press both SHIFT keys twice to get the machine responding again. Any message will appear only if you switch to Alarm (press ☐ A).

4 At the time set in the Alarm, the bleeper will sound seven to twelve times (seven long or twelve short, depending on whether the machine is switched off or is running) unless you have turned off this sound facility. The alarm bell symbol will appear at the right-hand side of the screen, and if you are using text (as with PipeDream or Diary) any message in the Alarm will appear in your text. Note that you may need to erase this if you do not want it as part of your text.

The Alarm options

The Alarm facility allows four useful options that are listed as BELL, ALARM TYPE, REPEAT EVERY and No. OF TIMES.

1 The BELL option allows the sound to be turned off – it is normally on. The cursor is moved to this option by pressing the down-cursor key, and the on/off switching is done by using the cursor up or down keys. The word will change between ON and OFF each time the key is pressed.

2 The REPEAT EVERY facility allows the same alarm to be repeated at intervals. The normal entry here is NEVER, but this can be changed by using the cursor up/down keys. Pressing the up key gives one second, with the time changing by one second each time the key is pressed. Pressing the down key gives one year, with the up key increasing this by another year each time the up key is pressed. If the down key is pressed when the display shows one year, the time changes to one month, and further pressing gives one week, one day, one hour, one minute and then one second. You can therefore set any time that you like with these up/down keys.

3 The No. OF TIMES column allows you to specify how many times the Alarm will repeat if you have specified a repetition interval with REPEAT EVERY. The normal setting is NEVER, and pressing the down cursor key gives FOREVER. Pressing again gives 65534 times, with the number decreasing each time the key is pressed. Pressing the up key makes the number of repetitions start with one and move up by one each time the key is pressed.

4 The change in numbers that these up/down keys cause can be altered by using the SHIFT or ◇ keys in conjunction with the up/down keys. Using the SHIFT key will make the numbers change by ten on each press of the up/down keys, and using the ◇ key will make the numbers change by 100. Figure 2.4 is a summary of the Alarm setting changes.

5 After an alarm has sounded, the bell symbol on the right-hand side of the screen continues to flash until the alarm has been cleared.

BELL ON/OFF	ALARM TYPE ALARM EXECUTE	REPEAT EVERY ↑ +1 unit. NEVER ↓ year ↓ month ↓ week ↓ day ↓ hour ↓ minute ↓ second	No.OF TIMES ↑ +1 unit. Once ↑ NEVER ↓ FOREVER ↓ 65534 ↓ − 1 unit.

Figure 2.4 Alarm setting choices.

■ SECTION 12

Alarm type

The ALARM TYPE option has two possible settings, ALARM or EXECUTE. The normal setting is ALARM, but by using the up/down cursor key, you can choose EXECUTE. This allows the Alarm to start a program running for you when the alarm sounds – and this is one instance when you might want to turn off the sound of the Alarm.

1 The EXECUTE action of Alarm requires you to enter a command in coded form into the message/command section of the Alarm setting space. This command, however, cannot be a word like Diary, since this would be taken only as a message.

2 To place a command into the Alarm message space you have to use the command letters B, C, D and so on, prefaced by the symbol # used in place of □ , the square. For example, to make the Alarm start PipeDream, use #D as the first part of your command. This can be followed by a few words that will be inserted into the PipeDream document.

3 For example, using #D Chapter 7. in the Alarm command/message space will cause the alarm to start PipeDream at the set time, and place the words Chapter 7 into the text. To start Diary, use #D. For more of these symbols, see Appendix B.

4 You can also use ~E to mean ENTER, ~I for INDEX and ~M for MENU to produce the effect of pressing any of these keys. For example, placing #D ~E Entry for today ~E into the alarm message space will enter Diary, take a new line, print 'Entry for today' and take another new line.

5 This *programming* of the Alarm commands can be considerably extended to allow for actions such as file loading or saving, but the commands that are required involve some knowledge of programming and have therefore been omitted from this book.

23

The Calculator

The Calculator popdown allows you to make a number of calculations when you are in the course of using applications programs, avoiding the need to carry or use a separate calculator. The calculator is not a programmable type, nor does it include 'scientific' functions, making it rather less useful for engineers. For advanced calculator actions, the use of BASIC is more appropriate, but the topic cannot be covered in sufficient depth in this book.

If you have requirements for programmed calculations, then you may find that you can achieve what you want with the Spreadsheet action of PipeDream (see Part 7) rather than with BASIC. There are, in fact, few applications for which you need to use BASIC unless your requirements are quite specialised.

The calculator allows the use of memory store and recall for ten stores, the provision for fixing the number of decimal places, and a slightly unusual 'swop-around' key whose action will be demonstrated later.

Numbers can be entered by selecting with the cursor (very time-wasting) or by direct typing, and the result will appear in the strip immediately under the title line. Numbers can be in ordinary or in standard/scientific form.

1 Ordinary calculations are carried out by typing a number, an arithmetical sign then a number, as you would with any ordinary calculator. You use the ∗ sign for multiplication, the / or \ for division and the usual + and − for add and subtract. All of these processes can be done by shifting the cursor and pressing ENTER instead of typing.

2 In each case, the result is obtained by pressing the = key or placing the cursor over the = sign and pressing ENTER. Direct typing is very much simpler and faster, and eliminates the need to use the ENTER key. Note that as you enter digits they appear on the results space, and if you press the ENTER key it has the effect of repeating the previous digit. You can delete a digit with the DEL key, or a complete entry with the C key, before you press an operator key (∗ / + − keys). Try the following sequences:

5.3 * 2.6 = (gives 13.78) (you can use X or T in place of
  *)
27.62 / 4.7 = (gives 5.88) (you can use \ or D in place of /)
21347 + 31604 = (gives 52951.00) (you can use P in
  place of +)
70412 − 36285 = (gives 34127.00) (you can use M in
  place of −)

3 All these arithmetic results are displayed correct to two decimal places, but the calculation is precise to nine places of decimals. The restriction to two decimal places is convenient for many financial calculations which are accurate only to the nearest penny.

4 If you need more precision, you can fix the number of decimal places for yourself. Place the cursor over the FIX label on the calculator, press ENTER, then type the number of places, 0 to 8 that you require. Numbers will then appear with this format. Using 0 will give whole numbers only. If you use FIX 9, then the number of decimal places will be whatever the fractions require, up to a maximum of 9. For example, with FIX 4, 1/8 gives 0.1250, but with FIX 9 this appears as 0.125. You can, instead of using the FIX label, press the F key on the keyboard, and then the number of decimal places, such as F4 for four places − you do not need to press ENTER.

5 Numbers can be entered in *scientific* or *standard* form, such as 2.7E5. Results appear in the more usual form unless a number is very large, needing more than nine figures to express in normal form, or very small, needing nine or more zeros following the decimal point. For scientific/standard form, see Appendix C.

Calculator constants and memory

You can work with constants, meaning that everything you enter can be multiplied or divided by a set number, or have this number added or subtracted. You might, for example, want to multiply each entered number by 0.15 to calculate VAT, or add a constant bonus sum to wages.

1 To use a constant, enter the number first, and then type the operator twice. For example, to multiply by 0.15 as a constant, type:

.15**

and from then on you can enter numbers and press the = sign to get the result of multiplication by 0.15.

2 When you use something like:

67.4 − −

to carry out a constant subtraction, remember that this means that what you enter is subtracted from this amount. In other words, if you used 2 − − and then entered 8, you would get − 6, the result of subtracting 8 from 2.

3 If you want to subtract 14.6 from each entered number then you can type 14.6, press I to change sign to − 14.6, then type + + for constant addition.

4 An alternative is to type 14.6 − −, use Y ⋄ x, either by typing Y or using cursor and ENTER, then = . For example, 14.6 − − Y 12 = − 2.6, the result of 12 − 14.6.

There are ten memory storage places allocated to the calculator, numbered 0 to 9. They are used with the StoM and RclM labels, or by typing S or R.

1 To store a number which is displayed, either by typing or as the result of a calculation, select StoM and press ENTER, then a digit for the memory number (0 to 9). To store 0.15 in store 1, type:

   0.15 (StoM ENTER) 1

or, alternatively 0.15 S 1 – typing the S for store.

IMPORTANT NOTE: You might expect, looking at the labels on the calculator display to be able to type something like 0.15 SM 1, and you can, but this will create havoc! You can type the Store and Recall as S and R respectively, but using SM will give negative numbers, summed numbers, and assorted mysteries, so do not be tempted by the capital letter M in the labels.

---

2 Once a number is stored in this way, you can make use of it in the four arithmetic commands of * / + and − . The stored number is recovered by using R with its store number, such as R1. For example, with 0.15 stored in memory location 1, you can type:

   30 * R1 = (and get 4.5)
   10 / R1 = (and get 66.66)
   .23 + R1 = (and get 0.38)
   .55 − R1 = (and get 0.4)

Note that using R1 or any other store number does not delete the number in the store, and this is not done by the C (Clear) key either, or by switching off the Z88. A number remains stored until it is replaced by another number.

3 If you want to zero all the stores, type a zero, then type S0, S1, S2 . . . and so on up to S9. If you are using a large number of stored numbers, you might like to work over a PipeDream or Diary page and keep a note of how you have used the stores on the page. For arithmetic of such complexity, however, it's better to make use of a PipeDream spreadsheet or a program written in BASIC.

Calculator percentages and conversions

The Calculator allows you to work in percentages, including addition and discounting of percentages. You can find a given percentage of an amount (like 15% of 147), express a fraction as a percentage (including decimal places if you like), add a percentage on to a number or subtract a percentage from a number.

1 To find 15% of 273, type 273, then the multiply sign ∗, then 15% to get 40.95 when two decimal places are fixed.

2 To express a fraction as a percentage, type the fraction and follow with the % sign. For example 547/875% gives 62.51. For this type of use you might want to type F0, fixing no decimal places so that each percentage is a whole number.

3 To add a percentage, type the number, the ∗sign, the percentage number and then % +. For example, adding 15% to 220.45 is done by typing:

220.45∗15% +(giving 253.52)

This is particularly useful for VAT work.

4 To find a discounted amount, follow the routine above, but with the − sign following the %. For example:

570∗20% −gives 456

The Z88 allows for built-in unit conversion between gallons and litres, miles and kilometres, miles per gallon and litres per 100 km, acres and hectares, pounds and kilograms, ounces and grams, Fahrenheit and Celsius temperatures.

1 To convert 37 miles per gallon to litres per 100 km, type the number 37, then U (or use the Unit label and ENTER) and move the cursor to the 1/100 km section. You will see the line change from:

MPG←1/100km   to   MPG→1/00km

to show that the change is from MPG to 1/100 km, and pressing ENTER gives the result, 7.63 litres/100 km.

2 This is the general method. Type the number you want to convert, then U for Units. Shift the cursor over the units to which you want to convert, then press ENTER.

3 If you change your mind about converting units, press ESC to get back to the ordinary calculator actions.

Part 3
The Diary

The Diary is one of the important applications programs of the Z88 and unlike the popdowns that we have looked at so far, it is a program that can be used, suspended and then used again. Unlike PipeDream documents, the Diary is a unique document which can be altered and deleted but cannot exist in more than one version in memory at a given time. In other words, there will only ever be one copy of Diary in the list of suspended activities.

The Diary, as the name suggests, allows you to keep records of past, present and future notes, appointments, telephone numbers and similar data. The Diary works along with the Calendar, Clock and Alarm popdowns and makes use of these popdowns to set the Diary date.

In addition, the data in a diary can be edited just like text in a wordprocessor. Diary entries can be copied from one year to another by making use of saved files, and we shall make use of the Filer for this type of work.

■ SECTION 16

The active day

An active day, as far as the Z88 diary is concerned is a day on which there is a Diary entry. In this first section, then, we shall look at how a Diary day is chosen.

1 When the diary is selected with ☐ D or from the INDEX menu, then the date for the Diary 'page' is the current date, whether there is anything entered for this date or not.

2 To enter a note or other data in the Diary for this current date, simply type the data. The manual shows neat illustrations making use of the TAB key, but you are not forced to work in this way. It is, however, a good idea to separate different topics by a blank line, as in Fig. 3.1.

Birthday: Sally Jane

Appointment: Dentist 14.15

Memo: Set VCR for 20.30 to 21.00

Figure 3.1 Typical Diary entries.

3 If you want to move on or back by one day, then press the ☐ key along with the cursor down or up key respectively.

4 If you have already made Diary entries, these days will be Active days, and can be searched for. Using ☐ with left/right cursor searches for active days, left for back, right for forward. You can find the first active day in the Diary with ◇ CFAD, and the last with ◇ CLAD. Figure 3.2 summarises the active day commands.

◇ CLAD	☐ ←	TODAY	☐ →	◇ CFAD
Last active day	Previous Active day		Next Active day	First active day

---

Figure 3.2 The Active-day commands.

5 You can enter or delete data in any of these active days, or in any other day that you select. Day selection can also be carried out by using the Calendar popdown.

6 If you call up the Calendar (with ☐ R) and move the cursor to a date, this also becomes the date for the diary. Returning to Diary with ESC will allow you to make or correct an entry for this date.

SECTION 17

Editing Diary entries

Editing the Diary is very similar to working with a word processor, and you can think of the ◇ key as playing much the same part in editing as the CTRL key of the PC when used with programs such as WordStar. The main editing key actions are summarised on the list just below the screen position on the Z88.

1 The normal action is text insertion, so that anything you type will be inserted into existing text. You can reverse this (for writing over old entries, for example) by pressing ◇ V. The action will stay this way until pressing ◇ V again returns you to insertion. The panel at the right-hand side of the Diary screen will show INSERT MODE or OVERTYPE MODE as a reminder.

2 Deleting is most easily carried out by using the DEL key for the character to the left of the cursor, SHIFT DEL for the character under the cursor, ◇ DEL to delete a whole line. ◇ T will delete from cursor position to the end of a word, and ◇ D to the end of a line. ◇ Y will delete a complete line and close the gap.

3 The spacing commands are sometimes useful. ◇ U gives a one-character space and ◇ N a one line space (compare CTRL-N in WordStar). ◇ ESL will move everything to the right of the cursor to the next line, since the ENTER key does not act like an inserting key. The opposite action of joining lines is carried out by using ◇ EJL.

4 Another useful command is ◇ S which will reverse the case (upper or lower) of the letter under the cursor and move the cursor to the next letter. You can hold this *pair* of keys (not just the S key) down to reverse the case of a word or phrase.

5 Using ◇ EMF gives the Extent of Memory Free for Diary entries. If this becomes low, you may have to delete some old entries in order to make room for others. The Diary system permits old diary data to be recorded as a file if needed, but this is rather pointless unless you can transfer it to a disk or to another machine.

33

Consulting the Diary

The usefulness of any diary system lies in the ease with which it can be consulted, and some computer diary systems are less useful and a lot less convenient than a paper diary. The Z88 diary system is very powerful and useful because of the ease with which you can locate entries even if you remember very little about them.

1 The cursor commands are used in order to move about the text in one Diary page – you are not limited to what can be seen on the screen. The Active day commands are used to locate the days on which Diary information is present.

2 You can also conduct a search for a word such as Conference. To find the first entry that contains this word, press ◇ BSE, Block SEarch. You will be prompted to type the word, with the 'standard' set of options:

EQUATE UPPER AND LOWER CASE .... Yes
SEARCH ONLY MARKED BLOCK .... No
PRODUCE LIST .... No
PRINT LIST .... No

and you would normally leave these as they are. Pressing ENTER will then find the first active day which contains the word you are looking for, along with the day and date.

3 To search further, press ◇ BNM (Block Next Match). If you want each and every occurrence of this word, take the PRODUCE LIST option when prompted and alter the No to Yes by placing the cursor over No and pressing the Y key. You can obain a printed version of the list by taking the last option.

4 The manual points out how the use of title words like EX: for expenses and MT: for meeting can allow you to pick out and list these items very quickly, even over a long period (the Diary is not confined to one year, only by the amount of memory you can spare for it).

5 If you are carrying out a lot of searching it can be useful to mark your starting position. This can be done by using ◇ CSP (Cursor Start Position). Subsequently pressing ◇ CRP (Cursor Restore Position) will move the cursor back to this point. If you mark more than one position in this way, ◇ CRP will find the marked positions in reverse order.

Search and replace

You can also combine the search for words/phrases with replacement. This type of action is rather more useful in a word processor than in a diary, and is provided, with some useful additions, in PipeDream.

One possible Diary application could be to changes that have to be made to entries that have been made for dates ahead of the present. Suppose that you have made the entry:

Phone Simpkins 0223 9990999

for the first Monday in each month. You find in March that this number has been changed on the grounds that BT don't like the look of it, and you now need to alter your Diary entries for April to December. This does not imply that you have to alter each entry individually, because the Search and Replace facility of Diary will carry this out for you.

1 **If you want to change the entries for the whole diary, proceed as shown below. If you want to change only the entries for April to December you will have to mark the block that extends from 1st April to 31st December – block marking is discussed in Section 20.**

2 **Press ◇ BRP (or use the menu). You will see at the top of the screen the message:**

STRING TO SEARCH FOR

which is an invitation to type in the item that is to be replaced, in this case the old telephone number. Do *not* press ENTER when you have typed this, and do not attempt to type anything that contains an ENTER keystroke. Press the down-arrow cursor key to move to the next section.

3 **The cursor is now located under the message:**

STRING TO REPLACE WITH

and here you would type the new telephone number (in this example) or whatever data you wanted to use. Once again, do *not* press the ENTER key. Use the cursor down-arrow key to get to the first of the three options.

4 The options are:

    EQUATE UPPER AND LOWER CASE .... YES
    ASK FOR CONFIRMATION .... YES
    SEARCH ONLY MARKED BLOCK .... NO

and in this example, you would want to place a NO into the 'Ask for Confirmation' line, because the item is one that is unlikely to appear by accident. Pressing ENTER will carry out the search and automatic replacement.

5 The screen will remain blank until the (comparatively slow) action of searching and replacement has been completed.

6 If you are converting anything that might be ambiguous, always use the 'Confirmation' option. For example, if you were converting each occurrence of 'man' to person under pressure from a new woman director, automatic replacement would result in words like persondate, chairperson, woperson, Walkperson and Opel Personta GTi.

7 Note that you do not have the same range of options in Diary as you have in PipeDream. You cannot, for example, replace a normally-typed word with one that is underlined or in bold type. This can lead to confusion if you are switching between one application and another.

Marking and moving

The Z88 Diary system allows you to mark lines or groups of entries in your Diary. Once marked, a number of operations can be carried out, such as deletion, shifting, recording, printing and so on. Marking allows these actions to be carried out on selected parts of the Diary rather than on the whole diary.

1 To mark a line in the Diary, place the cursor on that line and press ◇ Z, or with the cursor on the line, press the MENU key until the word BLOCKS appears in thick type, then place the cursor over 'Mark Block' and press ENTER.

2 To mark a set of lines, mark the first line of the set in the way shown in 1 above, then move the cursor to the last line of the set. This can be earlier or later in the entry for that same day, or it can be at a different active day either earlier or later in the Diary.

3 Note that all of the Diary entries between marked lines will be included – you cannot make exceptions. If you want, for example, to delete every entry between 1st August and 15th August, you cannot expect the entry for the 10th August to be spared. The solution, if you need to keep an entry is to mark that entry only, save it or move it (details later) and only then deal with the rest of the block.

4 If you decide, having marked a block as described above, that you need time to reconsider, then you can remove the marking by pressing ◇ Q.

■ SECTION 21
Copying and moving

A marked block can be copied or moved, and this allows you to carry out the placing of repetitive entries, a very useful action for items such as monthly payments or meeting regular deadlines.

1 Before a block can be copied or moved, it must be marked as detailed above. The marked block can consist of one line only (pressing ◇ Z once only, or of a section of the diary in which the starting line and the ending line have both been marked with ◇ Z.

2 To copy a block that has been marked, place the cursor where you want the copy to start. With the cursor in place, press ◇ BC (Block Copy) and the text will be copied to the new starting place. This is useful mainly if the text belongs to one day.

3 If you mark a block that belongs to a set of days, perhaps a complete week, and copy it to a new starting day, you will *not* get another week of entries. Instead, the whole of the copied week of entries will be copied to one single day.

4 Copying is therefore rather more tedious than you might expect if you want to copy text from several days into the corresponding days in other months.

5 You need to locate the day using the Calendar and then press ESC to remove the popdown. You then press ◇ BC to make the copy, followed by ☐ C to get back to the Calendar and SHIFT down-arrow to get to the corresponding date in the next month. This will have to be repeated eleven times to copy, for example, a 1st January entry to the first of each other month.

6 Remember that after you have made copies in this way the original line(s) will still be marked, even if you have switched off and returned after several days. You should make a habit of removing all marks with ◇ Q before ending any session in which blocks have been used.

7 The other form of copy is the Block Move, commanded by ◇ BM (or from the menu in the usual way). The difference between Move and Copy is that a Move will delete the original marked block. For many Diary purposes this is less useful, since the whole point of a Diary is to keep records of transactions.

8 A block can also be deleted, without Copying or Moving, by pressing ◇ BD. Think very carefully before using this command.

Listing blocks

Blocks that have been marked can also be listed selectively, either on the screen or on the printer. The listing shows the date and day for each set of entries, and you have the choice of listing the entire Diary (which might be time-consuming) or the marked block only. You can also opt to have the listing printed. Unless you make suitable choices, the whole Dairy will be listed to the screen.

When a screen listing is given, the screen shows up to seven lines at a time, and you are asked to press the spacebar for the next seven lines. You can, in fact, press any letter key, spacebar or ENTER, but not ESC or the ☐ and ◇ keys. Pressing ESC will stop the action.

1 Mark the block you want to list. This might, for example, be for a week that you want to review. Usually this will be so that you can print out a week's Diary entries.

2 With the block marked, press ◇ BL (Block List). You will see the options:

LIST ON SCREEN .... YES
LIST ON PRINTER .... NO
LIST ONLY MARKED BLOCK .... NO

and if you want to list the block you must convert the last reply to YES. Press the down-arrow cursor key until the cursor is over the NO on this last line, and then press the Y key (you do not need to type YES). The listing will then be carried out when you press ENTER.

3 If you want to abandon the listing even before you start, press the ESC key. Note that it is possible to convert the YES for List on Screen into a NO, and then press ENTER. This has the same effect as pressing ENTER if you have not opted for the printed listing.

4 You can search a marked block for an entry. Follow the general procedure for searching (◇ BSE) and then type a Y into the line:

SEARCH ONLY MARKED BLOCK .... NO

so that only the block will be searched. This can be useful for finding information in a block such as a VAT quarter, for example.

5 You can also carry out a Search & Replace within a marked block. Proceed as for the overall Search and Replace, but put in a YES for the Search Only Marked Block question line.

Files

The other option for the Diary is filing. As far as the unexpanded Z88 is concerned, filing simply means copying Diary data to another part of the memory. This can allow you to start a new Diary, or to extend a current Diary, rather like placing your old paper diary in a bookcase and starting a new one.

Filing also allows you to add into a Diary. You can, for example, copy data from the Diary of one year into a file, then copy back from the file into the Diary for the next year. Remember that only one Diary can be used at a time. You can also keep a complete copy of one Diary in a file, reading into the Diary program whichever you want to use. You could, for example, keep a Personal Diary and a Business Diary as separate files and work with either, one at a time. In such an application, you have to remember to save the current Diary back to the correct file each time you change to the other diary.

1 The complete Diary, or any marked block of the Diary, can be saved by using the ◇ FS command. You will be asked for a filename, and you should use something that will remind you of what the file contains, such as DIARY88.

2 You will also be asked if you want to save a marked block of the Diary. In most cases you will want to save the complete Diary, so this option can be ignored. If you have marked a block and wish to save this (perhaps items that go into the Diary each year) then you can take this option in the usual way, by moving the cursor down and pressing the Y key.

3 The Diary is saved as a file which is very much like a word processor file. In other words, the days and dates are not saved, only the entries and the positions relative to the starting position. This can cause problems when you are saving from or to a leap year.

4 For example, if you saved your 1987 Diary, in which the first of each month was noted, and then loaded this file into 1988 (a leap year), you would find correct entries for 1st January and 1st February, but the entry for 1st March would be on 29th February.

5 Similarly, if you saved your 1988 diary and loaded it back into 1989, you would find that the entry for the 1st March was actually placed on the 2nd March.

6 When you load in a Diary from a file, you are asked for the filename and also if you want to load to the cursor position. If you leave the answer about cursor position as NO, then the Diary data will load into the year (or other period of time) from which it was taken. Each day and entry will then be correct.

7 Problems arise only when you save a Diary from one year and load it to another when one of the years has been a leap year. This is not quite such a problem as it might seem, because the amount of data that you would want to transfer is usually small.

8 Another solution is to keep your Diary as a four-year Diary. Unless you make very extensive entries, the memory should be adequate even on the unexpanded Z88 machine, and one block of four years can be copied to the next four-year block without problems, since the leap year will always occupy the same position (until 2100, that is). For example, if you transfer data from 1988–91 to 1992–95 then the first year in each group is the leap year and the data will transfer correctly.

9 Files that you create from the Diary can be transferred to or from another computer (such as a PC) by using the methods that are described in Part 4 for PipeDream. This does not mean that such files can be used in other Diary programs for the other computer, but if you are not using a disk system on the Z88 then this can be a convenient method for long-term storage. The files held on a PC disk can, in addition, be read by a word processor for the PC.

Part 4

■ SECTION 24

Introduction to PipeDream

PipeDream is a large and complex program of the *integrated* type, meaning that it combines the actions of word processor, spreadsheet and database. Each of these actions will be dealt with in detail, and this Part is intended to introduce the terms and ideas that are peculiar to PipeDream and which you may not have met on other software for other machines.

1. No matter which application you choose for PipeDream, the work will normally be shown on screen divided into columns that are labelled by letters of the alphabet. Each letter refers to the column to its left. Unless you alter the arrangement, the column holds twelve characters.

2. For word processing purposes, the column ends act like tabulator positions. Each time you depress the TAB key, you will move the cursor from the start of one column to the start of the next. Similarly, SHIFT–TAB will move the cursor back by one column. The column that contains the cursor following the use of the TAB key is further marked by having a row of thirty-six very small dots rather than the twelve larger dots on the other columns.

3. The end of a line or row is marked by a small downward-facing arrow. On the Z88 as set up at first, this arrow will appear at the F column mark. The screen shows only the A to F columns, corresponding to seventy-two characters.

45

4 The arrangement of your line, using a dot to represent each character, is shown by the screen 'map' at the right-hand side of the keyboard. This is a useful guide, particularly if you can't see the whole of a text line on screen. The map can be turned on or off, or its size changed, see Panel later in Section 27.

5 A line of seventy-two characters is well suited to many purposes, particularly for word-processing on A4 sheets, but you can alter the position of the right-hand margin. This can be done by using ◇ H or from the Layout Menu. If, for example, you wanted to use 80 characters per line, you could type ◇ H and then type 80 when prompted for New width. For word-processing you would normally ignore the *specify Column* option.

6 A shifted right margin like this makes no difference to the appearance of the column letters A to F on the screen, except that the end of line arrow disappears. As you type text beyond the F Mark, your existing text will shift left so that you can see what you are typing.

7 You can also change the right margin by using ☐ right arrow. The position will be shifted by one character each time you use this.

8 You can, of course, set the right margin to a lower value, such as 40, by the same method. This can be useful if you are, for example, working so as to print on A5 paper.

■ SECTION 25
Slots

The space on a line that lies between two adjacent letter references is called a *slot*. This is of little importance for word processing purposes, but it becomes much more important when you make use of PipeDream for its other functions.

The width of a slot is the same as the width of its column, but there are slots in each row. You might, for example be working with six columns, which means six slots on the first row, six on the second and so on. This is why there are separate and different commands for moving to the next slot (the next occupied slot might be several rows down) and moving to the next column (you can move between columns whether there is text in the columns or not).

The standard slot and column width is the twelve character slot, referred to by the letter of the alphabet to the right. The maximum number of slots starts off at six, and this may be a limitation in many spreadsheet and database applications. You can, however, add slots up to a maximum of forty-two.

1 Always move from slot to slot on a line by using the TAB key to move right or SHIFT–TAB keys to move left. Some actions on slots (see Part 7) will fail if you use the ordinary cursor left and right arrows for movement between slots.

2 To add a new slot at the end of a line, type ◇ EAC (End Add Column). If you do this at a time when you were using letters A to F, then the new letter G will appear. The letters G to Z are used, followed by AA, AB, AC and so on to AP. The screen normally shows only slots A to F, however. You can add a slot at the left-hand side by using ◇ EIC, and this will cause the remaining slots to be relettered so that the first slot at the left-hand side is always slot A.

3 The number of characters per slot or column can be changed by using ◇ W and then typing the new number. If, for example, you wanted to use fixed tabulation stops of five characters for word-processing, you could type 5. This, however, will alter the number of characters for one slot only, the slot that contains the cursor.

4 The slot can be specified by having placed the cursor there by using TAB (in other words, the slot is marked out by the row of thirty-six small dots) and ignoring the *Specify column* option. The alternative is to move the cursor to the Specify column option NO, type Y to convert this to Yes, and then type the column letter(s). For example, typing Y and then J would specify slot J, assuming that this existed.

5 The alteration of slot size has no effect on the right-hand margin as used for word-processing, and in this application, the slot position act only like tabulation settings.

6 By making the slots of different sizes, you can achieve the effect of variable tabulation positions. You can, for example, have the first Tab at 5, then next at 12 and a third at 20, deleting all others.

7 To delete a slot letter, place the cursor in that slot using the TAB key so that the slot is marked with the thirty-six small dots. Now type ◇ EDC and the slot will be deleted. This is not always obvious, because all the remaining slots will be relettered and closed up as need be. *NOTE* that data in the slot will be lost when a slot is deleted.

8 You can move the cursor to the start of any slot (not just in the current line) by using ◇ CGS. You will be asked for the co-ordinates of the slot, and you can then type in the column letter and the row number, such as F2. Pressing ENTER will then leave the cursor in the correct place.

■ SECTION 26

Cursor movement

The use of PipeDream calls for a set of commands for cursor movement, and these are essentially the same as the cursor moving commands of Diary. The use of TAB, SHIFT–TAB and the slot movement commands have already been covered. Remember that the commands to move to the start or the end of a slot (◇ with cursor left or right key) refer to whatever is in the slot, and have no effect on an empty slot.

1 The simple arrowed keys at the right-hand corner of the keyboard move the cursor by one character left or right, or by one line up or down.

2 The use of the SHIFT key extends the movement to one word left or right, one screen (seven lines) up or down.

3 Using the ◇ key with the cursor keys causes movement to the start or end of a slot (for word-processed text, to the start or end of a line). With the up/down keys, the ◇ key causes movement to the top or bottom of a column (for text, the start or end of a document).

4 All uses of PipeDream depend on your ability to position the cursor correctly, so that you should try to memorise these cursor commands as far as possible. The reminder strip just under the screen shows the most common cursor movement commands as an aid to your memory.

Editing – the Panel

Whether you are entering text or other data, the ability to Edit is essential. Editing covers deletion and insertion and also the movement of parts of text, possibly one or more complete slots or a piece of text that extends from part way along one slot to part way along another.

There are two basic ways of working with text or anything else that is typed. The normal method is insertion, in which a character typed at the cursor position is inserted between any other characters, not causing any deletion of characters. The alternative is overtyping, in which a typed character will replace whatever character the cursor was over.

Whichever method is used, typing a character will place a character at the cursor position and move the cursor one space right. Holding a key down will repeat this process, and the rate of repetition is rapid. This and other useful details can be controlled by means of the Panel.

1 The rate of key repetition can be varied. Use the INDEX to find the PANEL, or type ☐ S. The first option on Panel is Auto-repeat rate, which is shown as 6. This is a measure of the time between repetitions, and increasing this number gives a slower auto-repeat. Decreasing the number in the range down to 1 gives faster auto-repeat, but a value of zero turns off the auto-repeat altogether.

2 The next item in the Panel is Keyclick. If you cannot stand the uncanny silence of the keyboard (useful for working in public libraries, for example) you can turn on a keyclick. This is the second item in the panel, and is dealt with by placing the cursor on the answer and typing Y or N.

3 You can also select Insert or Overtype (type O or I). You very seldom need to use Overtype, and examples are where you might want to alter sums of money that are of a fixed number of digits, or renumber the items of a list that has had an extra item inserted. If you make use of Overtype, you have to use ◇ U to create a space before inserting a character. During editing, you can switch between Insert and

Overtype by using ◇ V. Nothing will appear on the screen to remind you of which method you are using.

4 The Timeout figure is the number of minutes that the machine will remain switched on after a key has been pressed. The standard timeout is five minutes, but you can significantly save battery power by lowering this if you are in the habit of pressing keys only at intervals. Too short a time-out can be a nuisance, however, if you need to refer to paper documents before making an entry and then find that the machine has switched itself off. Switching on again, however, always returns you to whatever you were doing. On the machine I was using, the Timeout stopped working after a few hours use in each day, so that the machine had to be manually switched.

5 Sound is normally on, but can be turned off if you are working in areas where complete silence is needed, such as reading rooms. Turning this off means that you get no warning sounds with messages.

6 The Map display at the right-hand side of the screen can be turned on or off. With the map off, some editing actions are very slightly faster, but the difference is negligible.

7 The Map size can also be altered. The normal figure is 80 dots width, but you can decrease or increase this. It's useful to do so if you are working with anything that is markedly less than or greater than 80 characters in width.

8 The date format can be European (day/month/year) or American (month/day/year). Type E or A to alter this.

9 The set of options on the right-hand side of Panel affect transmission of data, and are dealt with in Part 9. The memory options at the bottom of the Panel should be left as they are until you have considerably more experience. The default device :RAM.0 can be changed to :RAM.1 if you have fitted the extra 128K RAM in position 1.

10 If you can't remember which letters are used for picking the options above, use ◇ J instead of letters like Y, N, A, E and so on.

Editing – working on text

The editing commands of PipeDream are essentially similar to those of Diary, but with several extra features. If you have little experience of working on text editing, then some experience with Diary will be very useful before you start on the more complex PipeDream.

· The PipeDream editing commands include the normal set, similar to the Diary commands, for working with text, and an additional set that deals with rows and columns so that the contents of individual slots can be worked with. This latter set is intended mainly to be used when you are using PipeDream for spreadsheets.

In addition, there are some luxury items that are intended for word processing use, but which do not necessarily appear even on some very expensive word processing programs.

If you use a word processor such as WordStar on another machine, you may find that some PipeDream commands look familiar if you think of the ◇ key of the Z88 as being equivalent to the Ctrl key of a PC machine.

1 As usual, DEL will delete a character to the left of the cursor and SHIFT DEL will delete a character under the cursor.

2 Using ◇ T will delete a complete word starting at the cursor position. Note that if you have placed the cursor midway along a word, only the part under the cursor and to the right of this position will be deleted.

3 You can also switch between Insert and Overtype by using ◇ V. This is a temporary change, not identical to the change in the Panel menu.

4 A line can be split by using ◇ ESL. This will move text under and to the right of the cursor to the next line. This is not the same action as ◇ N, which inserts a blank line above the line in which the cursor is placed. The reverse operation, joining two lines together, uses ◇ EJL. The cursor should be placed at the end of the first of the lines in order to use ◇ EJL to join in the second line.

5 ◇ S allows you to swap the case of the character under the cursor, and then moves the cursor one place right. Holding this key down will allow you to convert the case of a word or phrase unless you have turned the auto-repeat off.

6 The ◇ R command allows you to reformat a paragraph. This is used during word processing when editing of a text has made gaps in lines. The cursor is taken to the start of the paragraph, and pressing ◇ R will adjust all the words in the paragraph to suit the format you have used (number of characters per line, use of right justification, etc.).

SECTION 29

Rows and columns

When you are working with PipeDream as a spreadsheet, and to a considerable extent when you are using PipeDream as a database, you are more concerned with the contents of each slot than with a continuous text. For this reason, PipeDream also has a set of commands which are designed for editing slot contents as a whole for spreadsheet use. Unlike text, which is treated character-by-character, the contents of a slot is treated as one single unit (which it is).

Some of these commands will mean very little unless you are accustomed to working with spreadsheets, and these applied to PipeDream will be more fully explained in Part 7.

If you are using PipeDream only for word processing/database or only for a spreadsheet, you can make its use easier by specifying that every slot will be used for words or for spreadsheet numbers. This is done from the PipeDream options menu.

With PipeDream running, press ◇ O or select Options from MENU. You will see that the first item is Text/Numbers, for which you can type T or N (T is standard). Typing N makes evey slot available for use in spreadsheet mode. Remember also the use of ◇ J for selection.

You can, however, mix spreadsheet use and text use with ◇ ENT. If you are entering text, then pressing ◇ ENT will convert the slot that contains the cursor to number entry for spreadsheet use. In this mode, a number typed will appear on the top of the screen until you press ENTER. Typing ◇ ENT again returns you to text use. *NOTE* that the effect of ◇ ENT extends to one slot only, unlike the *global* selection of Text/Number from the Panel.

When you are working in spreadsheet mode, the normal cursor controls move the cursor from one end of a slot to the other, and the DEL key has no effect. You need therefore to use different editing methods which are peculiar to spreadsheet slots.

1 Pressing ◇ D will delete the entire contents of a slot when the cursor starts placed at the left-hand side of the slot.

		↓ ◇ EDRC		◇ EDRC used on column C	
COLA1	COLB1	COLC1	COLD1	COLE1	COLF1
COLA2	COLB2	COLC2	COLD2	COLE2	COLF2
COLA3	COLB3	COLC3	COLD3	COLE2	COLF3
COLA4	COLB4	COLC4	COLD4	COLE4	COLF4
COLA5	COLB5	COLC5	COLD5	COLE5	COLF5
COLA6	COLB6	COLC6	COLD6	COLE6	COLF6
COLA7	COLB7	COLC7	COLD7	COLE7	COLF7

After ◇ EDRC

COLA1	COLB1	COLC2	COLD1	COLE1	COLF1
COLA2	COLB2	COLC3	COLD2	COLE2	COLF2
COLA3	COLB3	COLC4	COLD3	COLE3	COLF3
COLA4	COLB4	COLC5	COLD4	COLE4	COLF4
COLA5	COLB5	COLC6	COLD5	COLE5	COLF5
COLA6	COLB6	COLC7	COLD6	COLE6	COLF6
COLA7	COLB7		COLD7	COLE7	COLF7

Figure 4.1 How ◇ EDRC deletes a slot and moves other slots up.

◇ EIC				◇ EIC inserting column		
COLA1	COLB1	COLC1	COLD1	COLE1	COLF1	
COLA2	COLB2	COLC2	COLD2	COLE2	COLF2	
COLA3	COLB3	COLC3	COLD3	COLE3	COLF3	
COLA4	COLB4	COLC4	COLD4	COLE4	COLF4	
COLA5	COLB5	COLC5	COLD5	COLE5	COLF5	New
COLA6	COLB6	COLC6	COLD6	COLE6	COLF6	column
COLA7	COLB7	COLC7	COLD7	COLE7	COLF7	inserted
						↓
COLA1	COLB1	NEW1	COLC1	COLD1	COLE1	COLF1
COLA2	COLB2	NEW2	COLC2	COLD2	COLE2	COLF2
COLA3	COLB3	NEW3	COLC3	COLD3	COLE3	COLF3
COLA4	COLB4	NEW4	COLC4	COLD4	COLE4	COLF4
COLA5	COLB5	NEW5	COLC5	COLD5	COLE5	COLF5
COLA6	COLB6	NEW6	COLC6	COLD6	COLE6	COLF6
COLA7	COLB7	NEW6	COLC7	COLD7	COLE7	COLF7

Figure 4.2 Using ◇ EIC to insert a new column.

2 Using ◇ EDRC will delete the contents of the slot that contains the cursor and move up the contents of the slots in the same column to fill the gap – see Fig. 4.1. The command ◇ EIRC does the opposite – it clears a slot, moving the slots below it in the same column downwards.

3 Using ◇ EDC will delete a complete vertical column at the cursor slot and below it, all the way to the end of the work. Using ◇ EIC will similarly insert a new column at the cursor position, pushing any existing columns to the right. See Fig. 4.2.

4 The command ◇ Y will delete a complete row and close up rows below that position; ◇ N will insert a row below the row that contains the cursor, moving other rows down as required.

Part 5
Word Processing with PipeDream (1)

The word processing actions of PipeDream approximate reasonably well to WYSIWYG – What You See Is What You Get. The main limitation is the screen size which forces you to work with a maximum of seventy-two characters at a time and a maximum of seven lines visible at any time.

This does not imply that you cannot use lines longer than seventy-two characters, because the text can be shifted sideways on the screen to show text that lies beyond the normal limits, just as it can be shifted line by line (*scrolled*) to show lines that lie beyond the seven-line limit.

The effect of this is that if you need to compare different parts of your text, you have to rely on memory, but the same is true of some word processing programs that cost more than the whole Z88 package. You can also, with PipeDream, maintain one line of text on the screen while you scan through the others, something that is not a feature of many other word processors.

The entry of text into PipeDream depends on using the cursor positioning commands and the editing commands, both of which we have looked at earlier, and most of which are familiar from the use of Diary.

In this Part and also in Part 6, we shall concentrate on the features of PipeDream that make it an advanced and useful word processing package. Note that if you have already typed a quantity of text, any alterations that are made in the layout can be made to affect the existing text – you do not have to start using PipeDream with rigidly-defined ideas about how the final printed page will look.

Since the ultimate aim of word processing is to produce a printed document, it may seem odd that the topic of printing is dealt with separately in Part 9. This is because the methods that are needed to use a printer are common to all applications, and require a set of commands that do not rightly belong with a description of word processing. Only the bare bones of printing are dealt with in Part 6.

In addition, many users of the Z88 will use the machine as a method of computing or word processing while on the move or away from home base. These users will probably wish to transfer their work into a PC or equivalent machine and work on it further, rather than printing direct from the Z88. The commands that are needed to transfer are remarkably similar to those needed for printing, so that both topics have been bundled together.

The screen layout

The standard screen layout of PipeDream for word processing is of the six slots that appear when the machine is first switched into PipeDream for the first time. This layout is not necessarily ideal for word processing use, though the seventy-two character line is well suited for use with A4 paper using a 12-point size of print.

No matter what appears on the screen as you type text, the layout can be changed later. You do not therefore need to learn how to alter the PipeDream layout simply in order to start using it as a word processor. Once your requirements extend to the use of a printer driven by the Z88, however, you will need to learn about layout. If you type text simply to transfer it to a PC to finish with another word processor, then the layout is immaterial.

1 The Layout options of PipeDream are obtained from the Layout menu – press the MENU key until this word is seen in thick (bold) print. Not all of the choices are important at first.

2 The Width command is ◇ W, and it sets the width of columns for word processing – this means that it sets the Tabulation stops. The column whose width is set is the column that contains the cursor. If you want Tab stops at 5, 12, and 20, then place the cursor in column A, press ◇ W, then type 5 and press ENTER. You then have to move to the next column, press ◇ W, then 7, press ENTER. The last stop is put in by moving to column C, ◇ W, 8, press ENTER. Figure 5.1 shows the reasons for using these numbers.

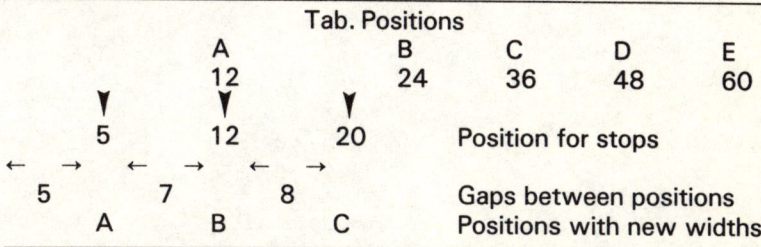

	Tab. Positions			
A	B	C	D	E
12	24	36	48	60
5	12	20	Position for stops	
5	7	8	Gaps between positions	
A	B	C	Positions with new widths	

Figure 5.1 Setting Tab stops – this is not like the scheme used on other word processors.

3 The position of the right margin can also be set. You can use the ◇ W command to make a wider last section (type the width number of 52 for a total line length of seventy-two) or move the margin by using ☐ with the right or left cursor key. You can also use the ◇ H command separately to fix the position of the right margin at seventy-two or whatever you want.

4 The left margin, as seen on screen, remains fixed unless you are working with multi-column displays. The creation of such displays has not been dealt with here, because it is unlikely that you will need it – if you want to use desktop publishing you are not likely to be using the Z88 for the final setting of text. The printed margin can be altered by using the left-margin option in the Options menu (press ◇ O for menu).

5 All of the other options that affect the page, and particularly the printed page, are set from the Options menu, obtained by pressing ◇ O or from the MENU sequence of PipeDream.

The other Options

The Options page should be consulted at intervals during the typing of a document in order to check the amount of free memory. This will generally hover at around 9000 for very short documents, but will diminish with uncomfortable speed when you are working on anything more than a page or so long.

The manual advises that you stop adding text when the amount of free memory reaches about 300 characters. This leaves just about enough space to work with the commands that will save the text to another machine, or, when it becomes available, to a Z88 disk system.

If you depend on transferring text to another machine, it is better to leave a generous amount of free memory, enough to save a PipeDream file in memory, since the transfer of text from memory is so much simpler.

We shall look now at some of the other options of the Options page. You move from one option to another by pressing the down or up arrow cursor keys. You can then change the answer by typing the appropriate letter, or by using <> J if the appropriate letter is not obvious. The selection is confirmed by pressing ENTER or by moving to the next choice. Return to the document by pressing ESC.

1 You can remove borders by typing Y on this line. This will remove the line numbers that appear on screen (they are not printed) and the display of slot/column letters at the top of the screen. The option is not really useful unless you are working with about eighty characters per line, as it allows lines longer than the standard seventy-two characters to be displayed.

2 Typing Y for Justify will give lines that are right-justified as well as left-justified, so that the margin line is straight at each edge. This looks neat, but should not be used on manuscripts intended for publication, as it upsets an editor's word count.

3 Wrap is normally on, and you would not turn it off for word processing applications.

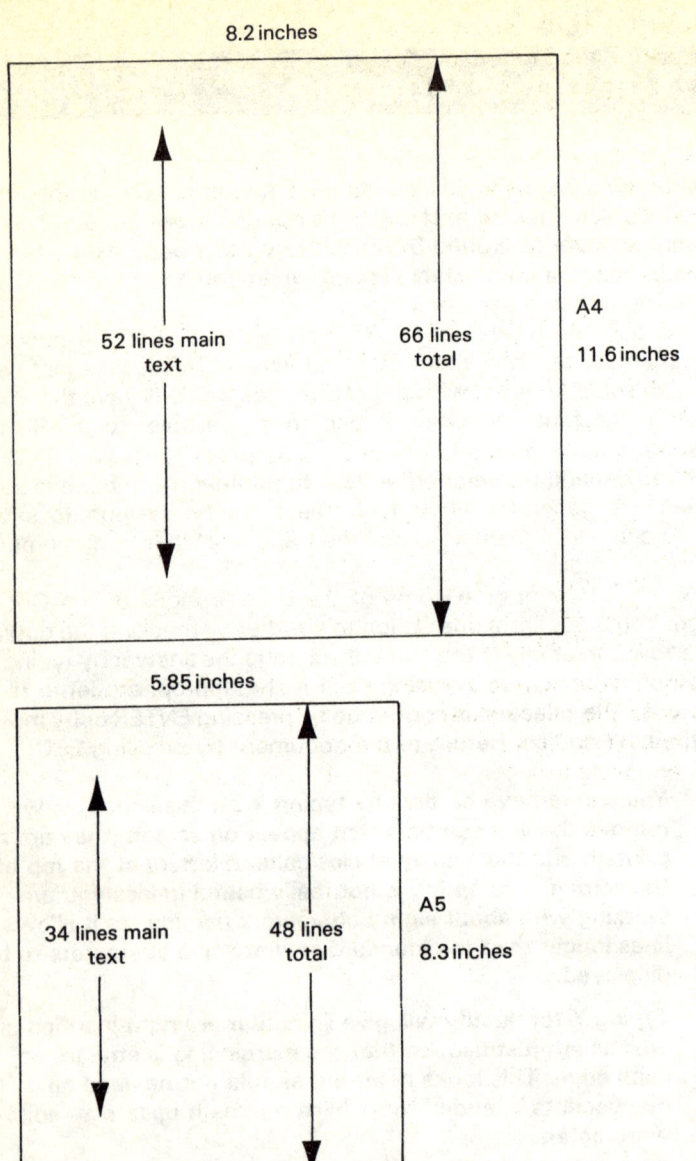

8.2 inches

52 lines main text

66 lines total

A4

11.6 inches

5.85 inches

34 lines main text

48 lines total

A5

8.3 inches

Note: Typical layouts only.

Figure 5.2 The lines per page used for A4 and A5 sheets, with margins.

4 The page length of sixty-six lines is suitable for A4 work. You might need to reduce this figure for A5 paper unless you were using condensed print. Figure 5.2 shows a line guide to page sizes for A4 and A5.

5 Line spacing of 1 is suitable for letters and some memoranda. For most article and book text, you would need to use double spacing, obtained by typing 2 in this position. The extra line spacing does *not* show on the screen – it appears only on the printed page.

6 You can type a starting page number, which will be 1 if not stated. This is useful if you are printing the document in small stages, as might be needed on the unexpanded machine.

7 The Insert on Wrap feature (R or C) is normally set to R; set to C only if you are creating multi-column text.

8 Several of the other items in the Options page refer to spreadsheet use. The next set relevant to word processing concerns margins. This allows all margins to be set, as illustrated in Fig. 5.2. You can also type in header and footer text (see Section 32).

9 Finally, if you have read in text from a file, the file name is shown in the information at the right-hand side of the Options page. This also shows the page number, whether you are using Insert or Overtype, and the amount of memory left free.

Text emphasis

In the course of creating text, you will need at times to emphasise words and phrases. Precisely what you can do depends on the printer that you use, but all printers can underline and print in bold or double-strike mode.

These effects can be obtained by sending coded signals to the printer, but the precise signals vary from one printer to another. PipeDream is set up for one very popular printer, the Epson, whose codes are used by many other types which are described as being Epson-compatible.

You can alter the printer-codes of PipeDream to suit whatever printer you use (see PrinterEd, Part 9), but in this section we shall concentrate on placing the codes into text. This does not require you to know what these codes are, and what is put into the text to carry out these effects remains constant even if you change printers and have to use PrinterEd to change the codes.

Printed examples in this section have been made by an Epson RX-80, with the PrinterEd program used to alter the normal print to Elite (rather than Pica), and using double-strike rather than bold.

1 Underlining is started and terminated by pressing the ◇ PU, (Print Underlined) keys. At each point where you use ◇ PU you will see the number 1 appear in inverse video (light on dark) while the cursor is on the same line. This changes to show underlining on screen when the cursor is moved to the next line, either by wrapping around at the end of the line or by pressing ENTER. Figure 5.3 shows examples of this effect.

This is a demonstration of <u>underlining</u> of words.

If the underlining is switched on,<u>and not cancelled, it</u> will be automatically cancelled when the ENTER key is used.

Figure 5.3 Underlining in action.

2 The number 1 is called the *highlight code* and it is assigned to underlining by commands in the PrinterEd program. The highlight codes (eight in all) cannot be put in by typing numbers, only by using commands that start with pressing the diamond key.

3 Each highlight code must be placed twice in the text, once where it is to start and once where it is to end. In addition, codes 1 to 5 inclusive will end when the ENTER key is pressed. This avoids huge amounts of text being printed in the wrong style because of the omission of a highlight code to end an effect.

4 Bold type is obtained using ◇ PB (Print Bold), code 2. Code 3 is called *Extended sequence* and does nothing on the Epson-RX printer, though it can be set up to give special characters, as demonstrated in Part 9. Both effects show on screen when the cursor is on another line. Bold type shows as heavy print and extended as lighter print. See Fig. 5.4 for printed examples of the use of Bold.

```
This is a demonstration of bold printing of words.
If the bold type is switched on and not cancelled, it
will be automatically cancelled when the ENTER key is used.
```

Figure 5.4   Illustrating bold type in use.

5 Italic print requires the ◇ PI code at start and finish, and subscript uses ◇ 3PL (L for lowered). These, like all the preceding codes will be cancelled either by repeating the code or by pressing ENTER. *NOTE* that not all Epson printers will permit italic printing. The printed result is illustrated in Fig. 5.5.

```
You can set into Italic print, which is also cancelled
by the <>PI code or the ENTER key.
A subscript looks like this.
```

Figure 5.5   Italic and subscript type on the Epson.

6 The remaining three highlight codes are *not* cancelled by using the ENTER key, only by repeating the code at the end of the section. Using ◇ PR (Print Raised) gives super-script, ◇ PA gives alternate font, and ◇ PE gives a user-defined effect – probably nothing unless you use PrinterEd to alter the code. Figure 5.6 shows these effects on my printer, and also the effect of using PrinterEd to insert a wide emphasised set of codes for User defined.

The **superscript** effect uses <>PR.

The alternate font has been set to Pica on my printer - you might want something different as illustrated in Part 9.

The **user defined** effect has been set to give wide print on my machine.

Figure 5.6 Examples of superscript, alternate font and user-defined text.

7 The PrinterEd file is also set up so that the £ sign can be printed. This can be very difficult with some word processors of US origin, but is delightfully simple with PipeDream, as Fig. 5.7 shows. See Part 9 for obtaining this character on other printers, or other characters on the Epson or other printers.

PipeDream shows the £ sign on screen and will also print this character. Surprisingly few word-processing programs can do this easily.

Figure 5.7 Printing the £ sign, very easy with PipeDream.

8 You can work with the highlight number codes by using ◇ PHI. This prompts you to type a highlight number in the range 1 to 8 (other numbers are unacceptable) and places the code into the text when you press ENTER. This can be convenient if, like me, you remember the number codes but always forget the letter commands.

9 You can remove a specified highlight effect from a marked block of text (using <> X, Part 6), by using <> PHR. You will be asked to type the highlight number, then pressing ENTER will remove that effect from your marked text. You can, of course, mark the whole of your text if you choose.

10 You can highlight all of the words in a marked block of text by using <> PHB followed by the number. This is very useful, for example, in changing a complete paragraph to italics. Surprisingly few word processors allow such actions.

Format

Your specified layout of text, in terms of characters per line, use of justification and so on, can appear to be upset by the actions of editing. In particular, deleting words or blocks (see Part 6) can leave large gaps in text.

PipeDream will fill in these gaps by closing up text, and can make the change from justified to unjustified, or the reverse. This is not done automatically, but is carried out paragraph by paragraph by using the reformat command.

1 Place the cursor at the start of a paragraph and press ◇ R. This will cause the characters in the paragraph to shift position if any editing has been carried out since the paragraph was typed, or if you have changed to justification on or off.

2 Each paragraph must be reformatted separately, there is no command to reformat the whole of the text as you might be accustomed to using in other word-processors, nor is the text automatically reformatted when it is sent to the printer. If, of course, you are sending the text to another machine for further processing, the format will probably have to be altered by the other machine in any case.

Other aspects of the formatting of text are the setting of text in the line. Text can be set so that it always remains starting at the left side, is centred, or set hard against the right-hand side. These effects require the use of the alignment commands.

1 Using ◇ LAR will align text against the right-hand edge of screen or paper. You can type the ◇ LAR command before you type a piece of text, or you can place the cursor at the start of a piece of existing text and type ◇ LAR to move it right. The effect is cancelled by using ENTER, so you need to use ◇ LAR in each line. The effect is useful for placing addresses, just to give one example shown in Fig. 5.8. Note that the words are not put into place until you move to the next line, and will be shifted left again if you move the cursor back to the line. This can make you wonder if the effect is working!

```
                              Tim Twitcher,
                               "The Nest",
                             Flocksville,
                                   Squaks.
This starts normally at the left hand side.
```

Figure 5.8   Using ◇ LAR to place an address to the right margin.

2   Using ◇ LAC will centre text. Like ◇ LAR, this can be used before you type the text, or on text that already exists, and must be applied to each line separately.

3   The ◇ LAL command forces text to the left, and is used mainly to prevent tabular material being moved by a ◇ R reformat command.

4   The ◇ LLCR command allows words in a line to be set to the left, centre and right of the line, using / to separate the words. For example, typing ◇ LLCR/left/centre/right would give the effect shown in Fig. 5.9. Note that the / sign which is used to separate the three sections *must* also be placed immediately following the ◇ LLCR command. You can use anything as a separator – a space ◇ LLCR Left Centre Right, or an asterisk ◇ LLCR∗Left∗Centre∗Right so long as the separating character is used for nothing else in that line.

```
left                     centre                      right

You can place          text where                you like
```

Figure 5.9   Using ◇ LLCR for left/centre/right positioning in one line.

5   You can remove alignment codes from a line by using ◇ LAF. This will leave separators like the / mark in place if you have used the ◇ LLCR command, so that you may need to re-edit after using ◇ LAF. To use ◇ LAF, you must place the cursor on the line you want to alter, remembering that when the cursor is on the line, the effects of centring and right alignment do not show.

Pages

Very often, your Z88 documents will consist of nothing more than one page – it rather depends on the length of your train journey. If you travel on Eastern Region, you may have time for a few chapters of a novel if you have expanded the memory of the machine.

For the longer documents, and also for some other types of documents in which topics are set out one to a page, you will have to give some thought to the way that a complete page is laid out.

1 The Options menu (◇ O) allows you to specify how many lines you place on a page. The standard setting here is sixty-six, but for A5 paper, you would probably specify forty-eight.

2 The lines per page setting that you need to use depends both on paper and printer settings. Most printers are set for a standard spacing of six lines per inch, so that a sixty-six line page corresponds to eleven inches of paper. This figure includes headers and footers (see Part 6) and any gaps. If you have a printer that is set to a different line spacing, such as the Continental 5 mm, or the alternative eight lines per inch that some printers permit, you will have to recalculate your lines per page accordingly.

3 As you type text, the end of a page is marked on screen by a line of inverted V's, in the style:

^^

and the position of this page end will change as you edit and reformat your text.

4 You may wish a page to end before it is filled with text. This can happen when you reach the end of a topic, or even after a few words on a title or introductory page. A page end can be forced by using ◇ EIP (End Immediate Page), then ENTER (ignoring the question).

5 Sometimes you need to prevent text from being split from one page to the next. If your text is almost ready for use, you can of course simply use ◇ EIP at the start of a split paragraph. If you may reformat several times, it is easier to use the provision in ◇ EIP to specify the number of unbroken lines.

6 For example, if you type a title for a new section, you might want to keep this and the next two lines together. Press ◇ EIP and type the answer Y to the question, then the number 3 (the number of unbroken lines, including title line). Remember to allow for double line spacing if you are using this. The screen shows ∼3 as a reminder, but this is not printed.

Files and filing

When you use PipeDream, the document you create is stored in one section of the memory, and you can return to it at any time from the INDEX by placing the shaded cursor band across the PipeDream entry in the suspended files list. If you simply select PipeDream from the INDEX list you will create a new document which can exist side-by-side (memory size permitting) with the other suspended documents.

In some cases, this use of PipeDream is enough. You can print the document and then ◇ KILL it from the INDEX list to make room for others, and for some purposes, such as memoranda, this might be sufficient.

More often, you will want to retain a copy of a document but not necessarily keep it suspended for further editing. You might also want to transfer a document to another machine, or to a Z88 disk when they become available. Actions of this type require filing.

Filing on the Z88 can be very simple, or it can be made as elaborate as it is on a PC machine fitted with a hard disk. Unless you have special requirements (very considerably extended memory and a huge number of files), you should stay with the simpler system. The advanced features of filing directories will not be dealt with in this book.

1 To save a file to the memory of the Z88, use the MENU key to move to FILES and select Save. Alternatively, press ◇ FS. You will be asked for a name. Figure 5.10 shows what you are allowed to use, and what I advise you to use for the sake of compatibility.

2 When you have typed the filename, you can usually ignore the other options, most of which are concerned with spreadsheet use. The only exception is *Save plain text* which can be useful when text is to be transferred to another machine.

3 The filename can also specify where the file is to be sent. If you do not do this, it will be stored in the internal memory, :RAM.0, or in whatever memory has been specified in the Panel options. No details of the Z88 disk system have been released at the time of writing.

A Z88 filename can consist of several parts, of which only one is completely obligatory, the main filename.

The main filename can consist of up to twelve characters. This must start with a letter of the alphabet, and should not contain colons nor full-stops.

An extension to the filename, consisting of up to three characters, can be added following a full stop. This extension can be used to distinguish the type of file. Do *not* use .CLI nor .SGN in your own filenames.

For the sake of compatability when you use a PC as well as the Z88, you should try to confine yourself to eight-letter names with a three letter extension, such as CHAP1.TXT, SPREAD1.BUS, README.NOW.

The Z88 also allows the use of a hierarchical filing system, meaning that files can be organised into groups, with a filename for the group. Each group can itself be part of a larger group, and the names in such a grouping would be separated by slash-marks. The group is a Directory for the files contained in the group, so that in the name:

WORDS/Chap1.txt

the file Chap1.txt is one of a set of files in the directory called WORDS.

The use of this type of filing system is really intended for large machines fitted with a hard disk, and there is no point in using it unless you expand the Z88 very considerably.

The filename can also be prefixed by a device name which starts with a colon, includes a full-stop, and is separated from the rest of the filename by a slash-mark. A typical name of this type would be:

:RAM.1/myfiles

and a device name can be added to names that include a directory, such as:

:RAM.1/WORDS/Chap1.txt

Since these extended filenames are very clumsy to type and difficult to remember, you should not use them unless you really need them.

Figure 5.10 Filenames – what you can use and why you should restrict length of name.

4 The specification of Device in the filename can allow a file to be sent *directly* to another computer (see Part 9), directly to the printer (not usually needed), screen, or other memory if fitted.

5 When you have saved a file to one of the memory units, you will see the name when you use INDEX to find FILER. If you find during saving a file that a message *File not found* appears, this is usually because you have specified a memory card (such as :RAM.1, :RAM.2 or :RAM.3) which is not actually fitted to the machine or which is not functioning. See also Appendix D on this topic.

Loading files

Loading a file means transferring the file (from memory or whatever other sources can be used) into a PipeDream document. There are two possibilities here. You might want to replace totally the document you are presently working on, substituting the new file. The alternative is to add the new file to the document you are working on, with the addition taking place at the cursor position.

You are not confined to loading word processing files, or even files that have been produced by PipeDream. You can load in a file that has been produced by the Diary, for example, or files that have been produced by PipeDream working in its Spreadsheet or Database modes. You can also load in files from other machines.

1 One problem that can arise when you transfer a file from another machine, because unless you have expanded the memory of your Z88 (which costs rather more than expanding the memory of an Amstrad PC, for example) you will probably not be able to fit long files into the memory.

2 This is not really a problem in the sense that it is asking the machine to do something it was not intended for. With the additional memory, you have the capacity to work with very large files of text, longer than you would normally need. A file for a large chapter of a book would be about 45000 characters, and this, though too large for the ordinary system, fits easily into the 128K :RAM.1.

3 The other main facility in the FILES menu of PipeDream is Name, the ◇ FC command. This allows you to name the document that you are working on in advance of saving it as a file.

4 You can load a file back into PipeDream by using the FILES menu, or with ◇ FL.

Part 6
Further Word Processing with PipeDream (2)

PipeDream is very easy to use, yet it is in no sense a 'cut-down' version of a word processor such as is often sold for machines in the PC class. Part 5 has introduced the fairly elementary uses of Pipe-Dream as a word processor, and in this Part we shall look at the more advanced features that it has to offer.

This still excludes many of the details of printing and the whole topic of the transmission of text to and from other machines, because these topics, which affect all aspects of PipeDream and also Diary, are covered separately in Part 9.

The important actions that are covered in this Part are the many block actions of PipeDream, the use of headers and footers, and the printing options. We shall start with the block actions.

Blocks

1 In PipeDream, as in Dairy, a block can be marked using ◇ Z, or by using the BLOCKS menu. Using ◇ Z once will mark a single line. A marked block can be cleared again by using ◇ Q.

2 Not all of the commands that are labelled as block command necessarily require you to have a block marked. By typing ◇ BWC when you have a document in PipeDream, you can get a printout of the number of words. This appears above the A column, and remains there unchanged until the cursor is moved.

3 Note that not all of the options in the Blocks menu are relevant to PipeDream. The Replicate command, for example, is a specialised type of Copy command for spreadsheets. It can, however, be used for documents in a rather specialised way.

4 Typing ◇ BRE asks you for a Range to copy from, and you can reply with a slot reference such as AI or a range like AI F7. For range to copy to you can similarly specify a slot of group of slots. Pressing ENTER makes the copies. This is sometimes useful if you want a single line repeated many times at some point in the text.

5 The more usual Copy command is ◇ BC, and this along with ◇ BM (move), and ◇ BD (delete) form the block commands that operate in the same way as their Diary equivalents. The explanations will not be duplicated.

6 Several other block commands are not used in the diary, or exist in forms that differ from their diary equivalents.

■ SECTION 38

Sorting

The topic of sorting really belongs to the Database use of Pipe-Dream, but it is a very common requirement to include in text material that is sorted into alphabetical order, and the ◇ BSO command of PipeDream makes this possible.

1 You might, for example, have a list of names that you have typed, along with ages, into PipeDream as part of your text. The form of the typing should be name, TAB, age so that the name and age are in separate slots adjacent to each other.

2 Mark this section of your text as a block using ◇ Z in the usual way. You have to take some care that the whole block is marked. If you forget to use the TAB key to move over to the age section at the end of the list, you may find that only the names are marked, not the ages.

3 Now press ◇ BSO. You will be asked to specify the column for sorting. If you have typed names in column A and want to sort in alphabetical order of first letter, type A here and then press ENTER. The word *sorting* will appear over column A, and you will see the names and ages put into alphabetical order of name (Fig. 6.1).

Zilliboy	22		Allanby	23	
Allanby	23		Bellway	25	
Xenon	24		Crossway	27	
Bellway	25		Deltam	29	
Teplon	26		Rioway	30	
Crossway	27		Sageone	28	
Sageone	28		Teplon	26	
Deltam	29		Xenon	24	
Rioway	30	(a)	Zilliboy	22	(b)

Figure 6.1 (a) A list of names and ages; (b) which can be sorted alphabetically.

4 If you now use ◇ BSO again, but specify Column B this time, the list will be put into age order, youngest first.

5 You can specify that either type of sort can be in reverse order. This means that names will be in reverse alphabetical order and numbers in order of descending size.

6 The option *Don't update references* can make even a short sort operation much faster and should always be used for this type of application.

7 In the sorting action as applied to words, upper-case and lower-case are treated as identical. Some sort programs do not do this, giving ridiculous results when some words begin with lower-case letters and some with upper-case letters. In such sorts, the upper-case letters are always placed ahead of the lower-case letters. The sort action of PipeDream keeps to true alphabetical order regardless of case.

8 If you have many columns and rows to sort, sorting can be a fairly lengthy operation – even a small number of items will take a noticeable time. Do not attempt to return to working with the document until you can see that sorting is complete.

Search and Replace

We have met Search and Replace actions previously in the Diary, but these actions are much more suited to use in the type of documents produced by the word processing actions of PipeDream. Because of this, the actions are considerably enhanced when used within Pipe-Dream.

1 All Search and Replace in PipeDream can be either on a range of columns (more suited for Spreadsheet and Database use), a marked block, a complete document, or even a set of documents. If you do not change any of the options that are given, you will search the whole of the current document, treating upper-case and lower-case as identical.

2 To search a marked block, carry out the marking if this has not already been done. Press ◇ BSE to get the search menu, and type the word or phrase to be found. Move the cursor down and type Y in the line : *Search only marked block.* Press ENTER to search for the first occurrence of this word. Press ◇ BNM to find if there are further occurrences. When the last occurrence has been found, you will see the number listed above Column A, in the form: '7 found'.

3 To search a complete document, leave the *Search only marked block* option set at No, and proceed as above. Remember that the Search command will find a word buried in another word, so that if you are searching for 'switch', then switching and switchback will also be found.

The ability of PipeDream to search a set of documents is particularly useful. The documents must be stored so that they are accessible, such as in the memory or in a Z88 disc system. The simplest method is to store the documents in the RAM memory.

Searching a set of documents

1 First, use PipeDream to make a list of the document filenames. This could be a simple list:

Chap1
Chap2
Chap3

with each name on a separate line. You can also use names
with device letters like :RAM.1/Chap4 (see Appendix D).
This list (called the listfile) should be saved using the *Save
plain text* option, and it must have a filename that ends with
.l (dot ell). Do not confuse the unfortunate use of letter ell
with digit one – the two look very alike in the Z88 manual.

2 Now open a fresh PipeDream document, and use ◇ FL to
load. Specify your list filename, which might, for example,
be MYLIST. You do not have to append the dot ell. The
machine will recognise that this is a list file and will load the
first file, Chap1 in the example.

3 When you now use the ◇ BSE search command, you can
take the option that permits the search to be through all the
files in the list. There will be a pause when each file is
loaded, but the search is made as if a single large document
were present. This is a most valuable feature of PipeDream,
and it would be extremely useful on a machine with a disk
system.

4 You can also carry out other PipeDream work, such as
editing, on the files in the list. Using ◇ FT loads in the first
file of the list, ◇ FB loads in the last. The command ◇ FN
gets the next file in the list, and ◇ FP gets the previous file.

■ SECTION 41

Search and Replace

The combined actions of search and replace can also be carried out on blocks, a document, or a listed set of documents, as described above. The simple use of search and replace is similar to its use in Diary, but the more advanced options, such as searching through the files in a list file, are not available in the Diary version of this command.

1 The Search and Replace command is ◇ BRP. You are asked to type the word or phrase (string of letters) you want to find, and the string you want to replace each with.

2 If you are looking for a word that might be contained within another, you can often separate the two by using a space following the word. If, for example, you are searching for cat (space) to replace with dog, you will not then get words like dogastrophe and dogacombs appearing.

3 You might want to cancel equating upper- and lower-case for some purposes. If you want to replace the name of your hero Bill by Tony (better image?), then keeping the Yes on *Equate upper and lower case* will give rise to Gas tony and Electric tony if you have such things in your text. Search and replace is a powerful weapon, and it can shoot you in the foot.

4 The option of asking for confirmation is useful if you have any doubts about what might happen. It allows you to confirm with Y or move on with N, or use ESC to stop. For a very large number of replacements, this could be tedious, and you might want to cancel it. Think carefully before you do so, and always check over the text afterwards.

Special sequences

All word processors have a search and replace action, but not all treat it as equally important. Quite a remarkable number of word processors, for example, cannot replace each occurrence of vital with <u>vital</u>, nor can they find where an underscored or bold type word has been used rather then the unadorned version.

In addition, it is very useful if a word processor can use search and replace to find such items as unwanted spaces and to replace them as required. This becomes particularly important if you work with a lot of text that has been transferred from another machine. You cannot always guarantee that such transferred text will not contain unwanted spaces or other characters, and an automatic way of deleting such effects can be very useful. See Part 9 for details of how text is transferred into the Z88 from other machines.

1 To search for a highlight number in text, specify the number by preceding it with the ∧ (carat) sign. For example, if you type:

   ∧1vital∧1

as your string to search for, then you can find each <u>vital</u> in the text, ignoring each 'vital'.

2 You can use the same method in the replace string. Using ∧2vital∧2 as the replace string, with ∧1vital∧1 as the search string will replace each <u>vital</u> by vital. This can be useful for changing emphasis, and if you confirm each exchange, you can leave a balance of underlining and bold type to emphasise these doubtless vital points

3 Using the carat sign in this way means that you have to adopt a dodge if you want to find a carat sign itself, or replace with one. The trick is to use ∧∧ in each case.

4 Suppose that you regularly miss the second letter of two-letter words and want to find all the single letters in a document. The sequence ∧ ? represents any single letter, so a search for ∧ S∧ ?∧ S (space letter space) will find such single letters with a single space on each side. Note that this will not find single letters with any other number of spaces – nothing is ever perfect in this business.

5 You can also use the ∧ # sequence to mean any group of characters (*other* than spaces). If, for example, you wanted to find all underlined words, you could use ∧ 1 ∧ # ∧ 1, with the ∧ # representing any word.

6 The characters ? and # used in this way are called wildcards, and the ability to use such wildcards greatly enhances the use of Search and Replace actions.

7 The other ∧ characters, as noted in the manual (page 93) are more suited for spreadsheet use than with word processing.

8 A very useful feature of PipeDream is that you can keep a line on screen while other lines of your document, allowing you a limited facility for viewing two parts of a document at once.

9 To do this, place the cursor on the line and press ◇ LFR. The line will be marked at the left-hand side, and from now on other lines will scroll as you move the cursor, but this line will remain fixed. Using ◇ LFR at any other position cancels the effect. Using ◇ LFC will fix column – this is not quite so useful for text work.

Headers and footers

The design of a printed page often calls for a title at the top of each page, with some other text, perhaps a page number at the foot. These pieces of text are known as headers and footers respectively.

PipeDream allows for the use of both headers and footers, along with page numbers, used on each page of the document. There is no provision, as there is with some word processors, for omitting the header on the first page, or for having odd-numbered pages carry a different header or footer as compared to even-numbered pages.

The default system is to place the headers and footers with no gaps (Fig. 6.2). This does not imply that the header will be at the top of the page nor the footer at the bottom. When a single sheet of paper is loaded into a printer, there will be a gap of about one inch between the printhead and the top of the paper, and the number of lines per page will determine which line is taken as the position of the footer. This can result in the footer being missed out if you have not allowed for the one inch at the top. The standard setup is for eleven inches continuous roll or perforated paper, whereas many users of word processors will want single-sheet.

1 The standard layout is for a total of sixty-six lines, eleven inches of paper movement. This allows for a gap under the footer of eight lines, and spaces, called header and footer margins respectively, of two lines between the header/footer text and the main text. This totals twelve lines, and if we use one line each for header and footer we are left with $66 - 14 = 52$ lines for text.

2 You can use this layout on A4 paper, whose length is about 11.7 inches. The Epson printer can start printing at about 0.7 inches below the top edge of the paper, and sixty-six lines added to this gives 11.7 inches, the exact length of the paper. The bottom gap of eight lines means that the last $1\frac{1}{3}$ inch of paper will not be used.

3 Figure 6.3 shows a layout which can be used for A5 paper in single sheets. This is for the same Epson printer; and has specified a top margin of two lines to make the 0.7 inches up to about one inch, with a bottom gap of six lines giving one inch.

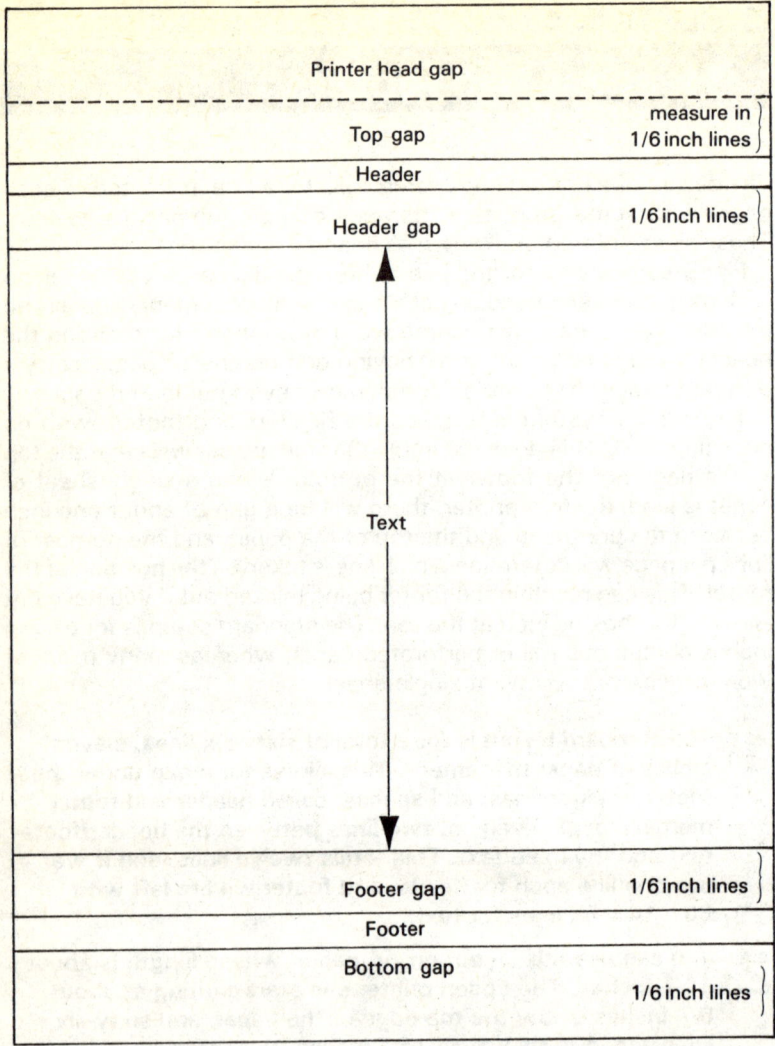

Note: 1/6 inch is standard line space, but many printers offer other gaps, typically 1/8 inch. The dimensions of gaps are always in numbers of lines rather than distance.

Figure 6.2 Header and footer positions.

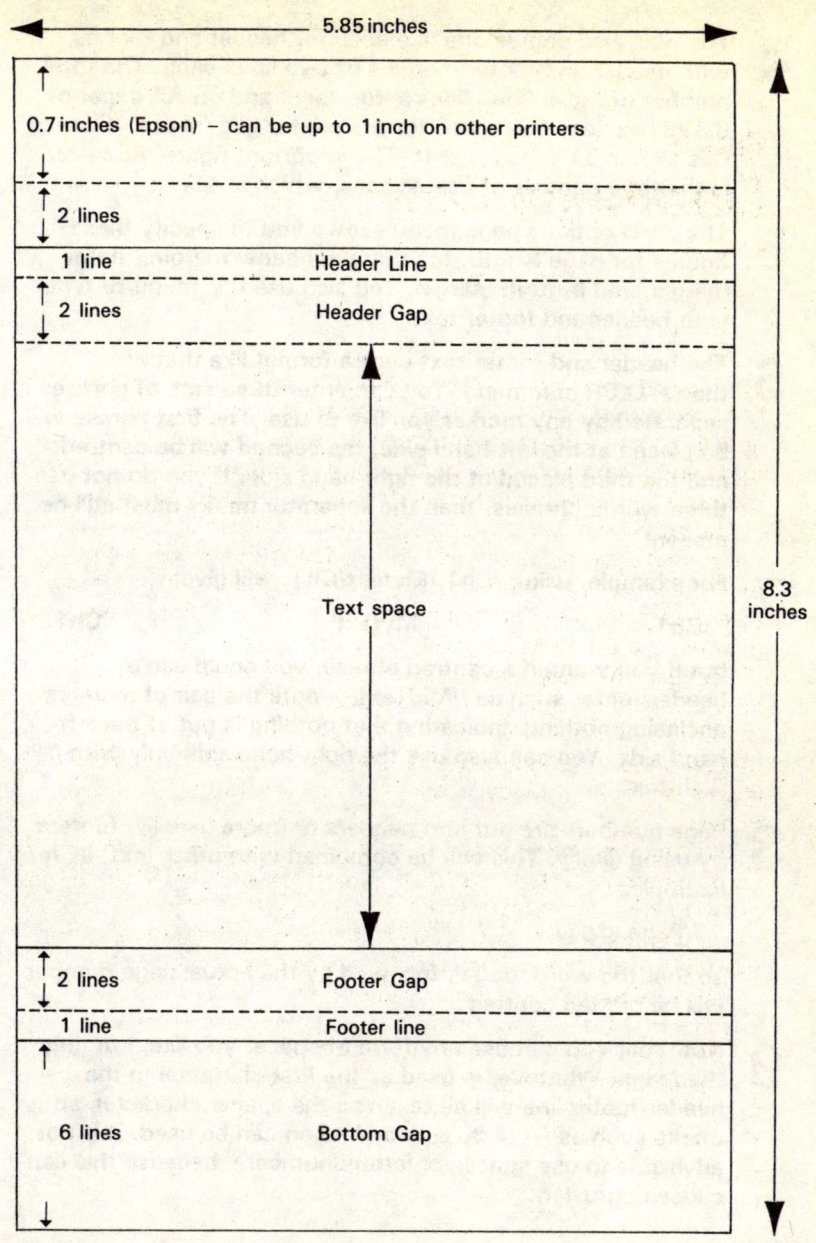

Figure 6.3 A page layout for A5 paper.

4 The plan also shows one line each for header and footer, with header and footer margins of two lines each. The total number of these 'idle' lines is fourteen, and on A5 paper of 8.3 inches, less 0.7 inches for the printer gap (about 45 lines) this allows 31 lines for text. The important figure, however, is the total number of usable lines, which is 45.

5 The ◇ O options page menu allows you to specify these figures for page length, top margin, header margin, footer margin, and bottom margin. You also use this menu to type your header and footer text.

6 The header and footer text uses a format like that of the ◇ LLCR command. You can enter three sets of phrases separated by any marker you like to use. The first phrase will be placed at the left-hand side, the second will be centred and the third placed at the right-hand side. If you do not use three words/phrases, then the separator marks must still be present.

7 For example, using /Ch1./Mytext/Ch1. will give:

Ch1   Mytext   Ch1.

but if you wanted a centred phrase, you could use a header/footer such as //MidText/ – note the pair of markers enclosing nothing, indicating that nothing is put at the left-hand side. You can also use the right-hand side only with /// Righttext.

8 Page numbers are put into headers or (more usually) footers by using @p@. This can be combined with other text, as for example:

//Page @p@

so that the word 'page', followed by the actual page number will be printed centred.

9 Note that you can use any form of spacer you like, not only the / sign. Whatever is used as the first character in the header/footer line will be taken as the spacer character, so marks such as / \ $ % & * and so on can be used. It is not advisable to use spaces or letters/numbers, because this can cause confusion.

10 When you are using headers and footers, the 'map' at the right-hand side of the screen shows the overall layout of a page. Very few word processors allow this to be displayed.

■ SECTION 44

Other setting options

The options page of PipeDream allows several other choices which will determine the appearance of a document. One important point is the left-hand margin.

1 Figure 6.4 shows a typical line layout on A4 and on A5 paper. The setting of characters per line is made by the right margin setting in the text (using ◇ H), but the setting of left margin (not shown on screen) is made in the Options page.

2 A common requirement is a fairly wide left margin to allow for binding. The left margin is stated in terms of number of characters, however, unlike the margins we have dealt with so far.

3 Suppose, for example, that we are working with eight inch wide paper. Leaving a margin of 1.5 inches at the left-hand side and one inch at the right, leaves 5.5 inches free for characters. The number of characters that can be fitted in here now depends on the pitch of the printed characters.

4 The common pitch figures are 10 or 12, meaning 10 and 12 characters per inch (printing is decidedly a non-metric business). If you are using 12 pitch print, then 5.5 inches of text amounts to sixty-six characters per line, and the left margin of 1.5 inches is eighteen characters. You would therefore use 18 as the left margin in the Options page, and use 66 as the right margin with the ◇ H command, since the screen always has a left margin of zero.

5 For 10 pitch print, 5.5 inches of line is fifty-five characters, and the 1.5 inches margin is fifteen characters. These are the figures that will be used in the ◇ H command and the options page respectively.

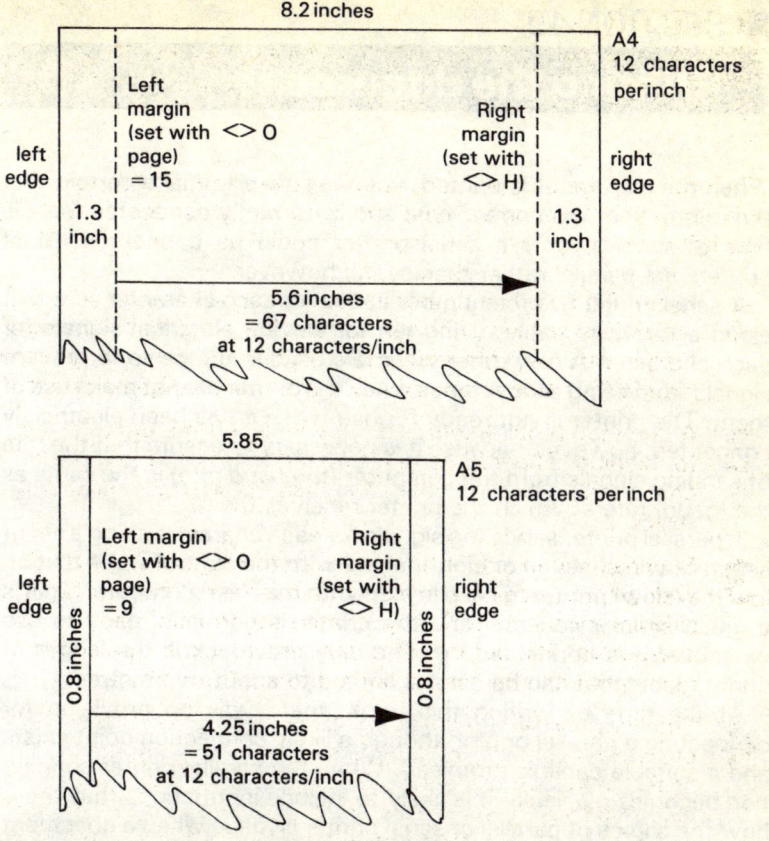

Figure 6.4 Line length layouts for A4 and A5 paper.

6 The options page also allows you to set the starting page number. This wil be set to 1 if you take no action, but if you are printing a document that forms part of a consecutively numbered set, you will want to set another number here.

7 If you have changed settings extensively, you can use ⟨⟩ BNEW to delete the document, and reset the document default settings. Do not use ⟨⟩ BNEW unless you are certain that you have filed the text, or no longer need it.

Printing the document

When the document is printed, you first have to make certain that the printer is of the correct type and is correctly connected. At the time of writing, only a serial printer could be connected. Most printers are parallel rather than serial, however.

A serial printer has the number-codes for each character sent to it along a two-wire cable, using ten (or eleven) electrical signals for each character. A few other wires are used in the cable to prevent signals from being sent at times when the printer cannot make use of them. The printer is not ready for use when it has been electrically connected, however, because it is necessary to ensure that the rate of sending signals from the computer (the *baud* rate) is the same as the (baud) rate at which the printer receives them.

A parallel printer sends the signals for each character along a set of separate wires (seven or eight), along with the control wires that allow the (slow) printer to keep in step with the (fast) computer. This is a much simpler scheme, and the printer is normally ready to use whenever it is connected up. The only drawback is the length of printer cable that can be used is limited to about two metres.

At the time of writing this book, there was no provision for connecting a parallel printer, though a likely connection point exists and a suitable cable is promised. When the parallel printer connection becomes available, it is likely to include instructions that show how the choice of parallel or serial printer is made when a document has to be printed.

The description of printing here is based on the use of an Epson RX80 which had been fitted with a *serial interface* to convert it from its normal parallel operation into serial operation. If you possess a parallel printer, or intend to buy a printer, make sure that the parallel printer adaptor for the Z88 is available. It is not worth spending extra for a serial printer unless you have other equipment that uses only a serial printer. At one time, most printers were serial, but the convenience of parallel operation has made serial printers obsolete, and the usual provision nowadays is of a parallel printer with an (expensive) optional serial adaptor if serial action is required.

1 The printer must be connected to its power supply and also to the computer. A serial cable is available from Cambridge Computers – I was able to adapt a cable from the old QL computer by changing one connector.

2 Consult the manual for the serial adaptor (or *interface*) for your printer to find out what the normal settings (called *serial protocols*) are. The speed (baud rate) of 9600 is often standard, or can be set by altering miniature switches on the interface. Other usual settings are no parity and no use of Xon/Xoff.

3 You now have to work on the *protocols* at the computer. Use the INDEX to call up Panel, and look at the set of four lines at the right-hand side. This shows the Baud rate of 9600 already set for you, with Parity none and Xon/Xoff Yes. Unless your printer interface allows Xon/Xoff (a method of synchronising signals), you should type N for this option.

4 Whatever protocols you use, the important point is that both sets should be identical. You cannot use different baud rates, nor different parity, nor different settings of the Xon/Xoff option. If an attempt to print produces nothing, or a page of garbage, the most likely cause is a difference in the protocols.

5 Once the protocols have been set, the printer can be used. Load paper into the printer, preferably using continuous stationery. Turn back to your PipeDream document, and press ◇ PO to print the document. This will allow you to specify a range of columns (useful for spreadsheets) or a range of rows (useful to print a selected part of a document, see Part 7 for details of how to specify rows), and the choice of pausing between pages.

6 For continuous stationery, you can leave the No answer to Pause between pages, but if you are using single sheets, you need to change this to Yes. You also need to alter the printer paper-end switch settings (see Part 9).

7 Pressing ENTER will then start the printing. If all is well, the document will be printed out in the way that you have determined by the settings of the PipeDream line and the Options page.

Part 7
Spreadsheet Action

A spreadsheet is a method of working with numbers that are entered and used to obtain other numbers by the application of formulae. You might, for example enter enter sale prices of goods and obtain the amount of VAT and the amount before adding VAT.

The importance of spreadsheets is that you can work with two-dimensional displays in which figures can be automatically recalculated when an amount is altered. Spreadsheets are generally illustrated with reference to financial uses, and this book is no exception. Their use, however, extends much wider, and they can have very valuable applications to engineering work, and any other field in which a result can depend on a large number of parameters.

There is no space in this book to do more than outline spreadsheet principles as we have outlined word processing principles. The examples will be short, since this makes them easier to try out. Once you know how the spreadsheet actions of PipeDream are controlled, you can make use of formulae that you have used with other spreadsheet programs, notably the SuperCalc type. Books of formulae examples are available for use with SuperCalc, and the methods can be adapted easily to PipeDream.

You do not have to keep the spreadsheet use of PipeDream separate from its word processing or database uses, so that you can produce a document in which all three forms of data display appear. It is often easier, however, to work on separate documents until the information is as you want it, and then combine all of them into a final document.

When PipeDream is used for spreadsheet applications, the concept of slots becomes important. A slot is the basic unit of the spreadsheet – it is called a *cell* in most other spreadsheet programs. The width of a slot is equal to the number of characters that can be typed into the slot, and the slot takes up part of a row. The position of each slot is described in terms of column letter and row number, so that slot C4 means the third column fourth row position.

PipeDream allows you to use up to forty-two slots per line and as many lines as the memory of your Z88 permits. Most spreadsheets do not require large numbers of slots per line, and it's advisable when you are working on a portable machine like this to stick to small spreadsheets. You can transfer spreadsheet data to another machine, and print it out as you require, but there is no guarantee that spreadsheet data transferred to (for example) a PC machine will work correctly with a spreadsheet program on that machine, because spreadsheet programs do not all use standard codes for their data.

Elements of spreadsheets

The setting up of PipeDream for a spreadsheet requires alterations to the way that slots are used. Some slots might be used for text (such as headings, day or month names), same for entry of numbers or the results of working on numbers (expression slots).

An expression slot is the general name for a slot that can accept a number for calculation or testing, or contain a formula. When an expression slot contains a formula (the *expression* of the title), then what is normally displayed in that slot on screen or in print is the number that is the *result* of evaluating the expression rather than the expression itself.

The first important action, then is to be able to declare which slots will be used for text and which for expressions. This requires some planning, and will be illustrated here with reference to a simple sheet that allows sales prices to be entered and analysed into pre-VAT price and VAT amount.

NOTE: It is important to use the TAB (move right) and SHIFT–TAB (move left) keys for moving from one slot to the next. Do not try to use the ordinary cursor right and left keys.

1 Figure 7.1 shows an outline of the very simple scheme. The first slot in each line will carry a brief description of an item. The second slot will then be used to enter a final price, and the third and fourth will show the pre-VAT price and the amount of VAT respectively.

Headings: Item, Final price, Pre-VAT, VAT
Final price is put in when using spreadsheet.
Pre-VAT price is Final price divided by 1.15
VAT amount is Pre-VAT * 0.15 (or Final price – Pre-VAT)
Amounts rounded to nearest penny.

Figure 7.1 Outline of a spreadsheet for VAT accounts.

2 We can now start to construct the framework of this sheet in Fig. 7.2. The first line can be used for titles, so that this is simply text entry. The real work is done in line 2. The formula for pre-VAT price is final price/1.15, and the VAT amount is pre-VAT price × 0.15.

Final price in slot B2 .... Entered from keyboard
Pre-VAT in C2 = B2/1/15 .... Expression
VAT in D2 = C2 ∗ 0.15 .... Expression

	A	B	C	D
1	Item	Final price	Pre-VAT	VAT
2		0.00	B2/1.15	C2∗0.15

Figure 7.2 The expressions for the example.

3 Slot A2 is left blank, and the TAB key is used to move the cursor to slot B2. This is taken as a text slot unless you command otherwise, and the form of the command is ⬦ X. Pressing this pair of keys marks this slot as an expression slot, blacking out the slot and placing the cursor centred at the top of the screen.

4 In this case, the slot will be used for entering amounts, and unless we enter something the slot will revert to text use. Type 0 (zero) and press ENTER, and you will see 0.00 entered in the slot. Compare this with the position and appearance of a zero typed into an ordinary text slot.

5 Now move with the TAB key to slot C2. Press ⬦ X to make this an expression slot, and type B2/1.15, meaning the amount in slot B2 divided by 1.15. Press ENTER, and then use TAB to move to D2. Press ⬦ X to make this an expression slot, then type C2∗.15, since VAT is pre-VAT price multiplied by 0.15. Press ENTER. In each case, when you press ENTER the formula disappears from the top of the screen and the amount 0.00 appears in the slot concerned.

Item	Final price	Pre-VAT	VAT
software	27.50	23.91	3.59
cable	44.60	38.78	5.82
modem	103.40	89.91	13.49
tools	35.70	31.04	4.66
	0.00	0.00	0.00
	0.00	0.00	0.00
	0.00	0.00	0.00
	0.00	0.00	0.00
	0.00	0.00	0.00
	0.00	0.00	0.00
	0.00	0.00	0.00
	0.00	0.00	0.00
	0.00	0.00	0.00
	0.00	0.00	0.00
	0.00	0.00	0.00
	0.00	0.00	0.00
	0.00	0.00	0.00
	0.00	0.00	0.00

Figure 7.3 A few items entered into the simple spreadsheet.

6 This concludes line 2. If you move the cursor along the line, always using TAB or SHIFT–TAB, you will see the formula for a slot displayed at the top of the screen (above slot A) for the slot that contains the cursor. You could, if you had time, then fill in each other slot in the same way.

7 It is much quicker, however, to use the ◇ BRE replicate command. Press ◇ BRE, and for Range to copy from enter B2 D2, meaning all the slots from B2 to D2 inclusive. For Range to copy to, type B3 C20. This has the effect of making a copy of slots B2 to D2 in rows 3 to 20. The copy is not a carbon-copy, however.

8 When a set of slots is replicated in this way, slot references are updated. In plain English, this means that the reference in the formula to B2 that we put into C2, will be converted to a reference to B3 to be used in C3, and so on. This ensures that the action of each line will be the same as the action of the first line, but with different quantities used.

9 Once the replication is complete, you can start entering items – Fig. 7.3 shows a few items entered and the resulting spreadsheet printed out. The headings are not well placed, but these can be edited into better positions now that some quantities have been put in. Note that all of the unused slots are displayed.

10 Note that if you can't remember a slot reference, you can place the cursor over that slot and type ◇ K to insert the slot reference into the expression you are typing.

Details of display

Before we look at more elaborate spreadsheets and methods, we can improve the presentation of the example. Since this is a simple example, it's easier to improve the appearance than it would be if we had started with a more elaborate system.

1 The first point is that the numbers are amounts of money, but no currency sign has been included. We need to put in a pound sign just ahead of each number item. The pound sign is called a *leading character*, and is put in using ◇ LCL.

2 Place the cursor at the start of B2 (remember to use TAB, not the arrowed keys). Press ◇ X to signify that you are going to work on the expression, and then type ◇ LCL. On pressing ENTER, you will see the pound sign placed into position just ahead of the first digit. Repeat this for C2 and D2.

3 You can now replicate again to put the pound sign into all of the other slots that require it. If you need to use a different currency character or characters, use ◇ O to get to the options page, and select Lead chs. to alter the £ sign to $, Sch, FF or whatever you want.

4 The printout in Fig.7.3 showed the set of empty rows. This is not necessary because the Print options allow you to select rows to print. This form of selection, however, is not the simple range form that we have used so far. Instead, you have to type a formula following Y (ignore the manual's reference to the down-cursor key).

5 The formula has to be something whose result is either True or False. For example, if you typed: b2 = 0, this would print out all the rows in which the entered number was zero. We want the opposite, so we type: b2 <> 0, meaning b2 *not* zero (the <> sign means *not* equal to). This will give the printout shown in Fig.7.4 – but note that the headings are missing. This is because b2 will be zero in the headings, since these are text slots.

```
software        £27.50          £23.91          £3.59
cable           £44.60          £38.78          £5.82
modem          £103.40          £89.91         £13.49
tools           £35.70          £31.04          £4.66
```

Figure 7.4 A selective printout which has omitted headers.

```
Item          Final price     Pre-VAT              VAT
software        £27.50          £23.91          £3.59
cable           £44.60          £38.78          £5.82
modem          £103.40          £89.91         £13.49
tools           £35.70          £31.04          £4.66
```

Figure 7.5 Including the headers but omitting the zero entry lines.

```
cable           £44.60          £38.78          £5.82
modem          £103.40          £89.91         £13.49
tools           £35.70          £31.04          £4.66
```

Figure 7.6 Selecting some lines to print.

6 The most satisfactory formula is ROW < 6, meaning row number less than six. This is true if the row number is 1 to 5, and this produces the printout shown in Fig. 7.5. If you want to print a more limited range, you can use a formula such as ROW < 6 & ROW > 2, as illustrated in Fig. 7.6. In this formula, the & sign means *and* so that the formula gives a true result if the row number is less than 6 and also greater than 2. This will print rows 3, 4 and 5 only.

7 The minus sign is usually shown as −, but for accountancy purposes you can use brackets, like (£3,415.66) by specifying this in the Options page (press ◇ O).

8 Signs such as £ and % can be removed with ◇ LDF.

101

Summing columns

The simple example shown so far uses its rows independently, showing the results for an entry on the same line. It would obviously be useful after a set of entries to find a sum for each column. This requires alterations to the last row.

1 Move the cursor to a suitable row: column A. In the example of Fig. 7.7, I have deleted rows 8 onwards, and used row 7. The word Total has been typed here.

2 Use TAB to move to column B, 7B in this case. Press ◇ X and then type the expression: sum (b2 b6) to mean that this slot should contain the sum of the contents of b2 to b6, all the selling price figures.

3 Carry out the same action for the C columns and the D columns. In fact, you will see these figures change once the B column has been changed, but because of the rounding to two decimal places it is more satisfactory to make an independent sum of the figures. The result is as shown in Fig. 7.7.

4 Look at this closely. You will see that the total VAT is £27.55, which is not equal to the sum of the figures above (which would be £27.56). This is because each figure is rounded to two places of decimals for display purposes, but held in memory with nine-figure precision. The result of the addition is the result of adding these amounts, then rounding to two decimal places.

Item	Final price	Pre-VAT	VAT
software	£27.50	£23.91	£3.59
cable	£44.60	£38.78	£5.82
modem	£103.40	£89.91	£13.49
tools	£35.70	£31.04	£4.66
	£0.00	£0.00	£0.00
Total	£211.20	£183.65	£27.55

Figure 7.7 Adding totals at the bottom of the columns.

5 The total is normally the amount you most need to be precise. You can, if you need, display with more places of decimals by using the Options page, moving to the Decimal places entry, and then specifying the number of decimal places you want to use. Another method is to use <> LDP followed by typing the number of decimal places (or free format) but this affects only the slot in which the cursor is placed.

6 The example shows the total line as row 7, but this is not necessary. You could, for example, have created a spread-sheet of 50 rows and placed the total on row 50. Even if only ten rows had been entered, you could then print out the rows that contained entries and the row containing the total. This could be done with the condition:

ROW = 50 | ROW = 1 | B1 <> 0

meaning that printing will be done if the row is 1 or if the row is 50 or if the value in column B is not zero. The value B1 is given, but the row value is updated as the printing proceeds. The | sign means OR, and when you type a long condition like this, the first part will disappear as you type the last part.

■ SECTION 49

Saving and loading

A PipeDream spreadsheet can be saved to the same devices (memory, disks when available, or to other machines) as can be used with PipeDream word-processed documents. Similarly, a spreadsheet that has been created earlier can be saved, and it is possible to transfer a spreadsheet from another machine if its form is compatible.

A spreadsheet will probably be compatible if it is described as being in ASCII form. If you are working only with PipeDream, the distinction is not important because PipeDream treats all of its files as equivalent.

1 To save a spreadsheet file, press ◇ FS. You will be prompted for a name, and if you want to save the whole spreadsheet, you can ignore the other options.

2 You can opt to save only a range of columns or rows. A range of columns is denoted by the letters, such as A F. The range of rows follows the same rules as for printing, using an expression which will be true or false.

3 If the spreadsheet is saved in the normal way, it still contains its formulae expressions, so that when loaded into another PipeDream document it will still behave as a spreadsheet – if you add another row, for example, the calculations will still be automatic provided the replicate commands is used.

4 If the spreadsheet is saved as plain text, it will *not* load back into a PipeDream document in its correct form, but as a set of items, one per line which can be reformatted as shown in Fig. 7.8. This is the formula form of the spreadsheet, not the form containing the numbers.

```
Item        Final price    Pre-VAT        VAT
software 27.5 B2/1.15 C2*.15 cable 44.6 B3/1.15 C3*.15
modem 103.4 B4/1.15 C4*.15 tools 35.7 B5/1.15 C5*.15   0 B6/1.15 C6*.15
Total sum(B2B6) sum(C2C6) sum(D2D6)
```

Figure 7.8 The sheet saved as plain text, loaded as normal.

```
  Item          Final price      Pre-VAT            VAT
software        27.5             B2/1.15            C2*.15
cable           44.6             B3/1.15            C3*.15
modem           103.4            B4/1.15            C4*.15
tools           35.7             B5/1.15            C5*.15
                0                B6/1.15            C6*.15
Total           sum(B2B6)        sum(C2C6)          sum(D2D6)
```

Figure 7.9 The sheet saved as plain text, loaded as plain text.

```
%OP%DP2 %CO:A,12,72% Item    Final price Pre-VAT VAT
software cable modem tools

Total
%CO:B,12,60%
%V%%R%%LC%27.5
%V%%R%%LC%44.6
%V%%R%%LC%103.4
%V%%R%%LC%35.7
%V%%R%%LC%0
%V%%R%%LC%sum(B2B6)
%CO:C,12,48%
%V%%R%%LC%B2/1.15
%V%%R%%LC%B3/1.15
%V%%R%%LC%B4/1.15
%V%%R%%LC%B5/1.15
%V%%R%%LC%B6/1.15
%V%%R%%LC%sum(C2C6)
%CO:D,12,36%
%V%%R%%LC%C2*.15
%V%%R%%LC%C3*.15
%V%%R%%LC%C4*.15
%V%%R%%LC%C5*.15
%V%%R%%LC%C6*.15
%V%%R%%LC%%D3%sum(D2D6)
%CO:E,12,24%
%CO:F,12,12%
```

Figure 7.10 The sheet saved as normal, loaded as plain text.

5 If the spreadsheet saved as plain text is also loaded as plain text, the result is shown in Fig.7.9 – this is a neater form of the plan for the sheet, showing expressions and entered numbers but not calculations. Figure 7.10 shows what the same sheet looks like saved in normal form but loaded back as plain text. You can therefore work with your PipeDream spreadsheet in a variety of forms either to show results or how the sheet is constructed.

Replication and slot references

The replication of spreadsheet quantities is a very important point, because without this facility much of the work on spreadsheets would be hopelessly repetitive. The value of replication is that references to slots are updated, so that a reference to D2 in line 2 becomes a reference to D3 in line 3.

This is not always desired, and PipeDream, like other spreadsheets, has a command which will 'freeze' a reference, making it the same in each application.

The principles of replication are well illustrated in the manual, and there is no point in repeating them here. Instead, we shall concentrate on aspects that are not so extensively or so graphically illustrated.

1 A slot reference can be fixed by using the $ sign. This can be placed ahead of the column letter to fix the column, or ahead of the row number to fix that, or ahead of both.

2 For example, if you specified in a slot the expression: $a5, this would mean that the quantity would be whatever was in column a of whatever row was used. If you specified A5, then the quantity used would be the one in A5, no matter what row this was replicated to. Using a$5 would fix the row number as 5 though allowing the column letter to change.

3 These fixed slot references can also be used in the Print and Save commands to specify single slot positions.

4 If you refer to a slot whose contents have been deleted this is likely to cause quantities in other slots to change to zero. You may also get a message about division by zero if a quantity has been divided by the contents of the deleted slot, such as 25/B2.

5 If you delete the slot itself, using ◇ Z and ◇ BD, then slots that depend on it will give the message *Bad slot*, and slots that refer to a Bad slot will show the word *Propagated*. If you move the cursor to a Bad slot you will see the expression marked with a % sign to show the deleted slot. There is no mark on the formula for a propagated error.

6 You can convert between expression entry and text entry with ◇ ENT. If you have entered a number without converting the slot to an expression slot, then ◇ ENT will make the conversion. If you use ◇ ENT on a slot that contains an expression, the expression (such as B2✱5) will appear rather than the *result* of the expression. If the slot is small, you may see only a small part of an expression and you will need to widen the slot using ◇ W to see the whole of the expression.

7 The ◇ K command has an effect that is sometimes useful. When you use ◇ X to edit an expression, the cursor in the slot can be moved to another slot. Pressing ◇ K will then put the co-ordinates of that slot into your expression.

■ SECTION 51

Expressions (1)

The expression is the heart of the spreadsheet, and the use of spreadsheets depends on your ability to formulate the necessary expressions. This is a matter of practice, though you can buy books of ready-made expressions, and for the popular spreadsheets like SuperCalc, you can even buy ready-made spreadsheets for various purposes, mostly financial.

The idea of the expression is much more flexible than a strict mathematical definition, because a PipeDream expression can consist of numbers or of text (a string expression). A string used as an expression in an expression slot must be surrounded by quotes (the '' mark), and the result of an expression can be a number or a string.

If you have no experience of spreadsheets, the logic that underlies the expressions is likely to be more difficult than the expressions themselves. A text that deals with the use of spreadsheets generally will help, and this and the following sections will deal with examples which in conjunction with pages 130–39 of the manual should assist you in learning by practice.

So far, the example that has been used has worked with very short expressions which could be accommodated in the standard twelve-character slot. For more advanced work, you might need to use considerably wider slots. If you do not widen the slot, an expression will spill over from one slot into the next.

1 The use of strings allows messages to be displayed. Take a look at the printout in Fig.7.11. In this example, a set of names and scores has been displayed with a Pass/Fail message in the third column. The message has been delivered by using the IF test of the PipeDream spreadsheet.

```
Name of candidate        score        Comments
Atkins, Tommy            29.00            Fail
Berry,R.I.P.E.           45.00            Pass
Cotton, R.L.             63.00            Pass
Delta, B.C.              16.00            Fail
Epsilon, F. Space        31.00            Pass
```

Figure 7.11 Using strings, in this case Pass/Fail comments.

2 The expression for C2 is:

   IF(B2 < 30, "Fail", "Pass")

which contains a condition (must be True or False), a True output and a False output. If the content of the B2 column slot of a row contains a number less than 30, then the condition B2 < 30 is True, and the string "Fail" is printed, otherwise "Pass" is printed. We might have used the condition B2 < = 30, meaning B2 less than 30 or equal to 30. Note that the strings are enclosed in quotes, but are not printed with these quotes.

3 *IMPORTANT POINT*: Though the manual does not mention this explicitly, only an expression slot can be tested using a number in this way. This applies also to other forms of selection, such as selecting rows to print. A text slot can be tested for strings, meaning words or numbers surrounded by quotes, so that the test:

   IF(B2 = "30", "Fail", "Pass")

could be used if the slots were text slots. Do not attempt to test for the absence of text, using IF (C4 = " ", ,) because this does not work.

4 A test like this can be carried out on a string as well as on a number. You can use tests that start IF(B2 = "Mr." or IF (C2 <> "mm" to determine the contents of some other slot. You can make the test operate on an unchanging slot by using %B%2, so that the first entry in a set will determine what is used thereafter.

110

Expressions (2)

The list of expressions in the manual contains tests and functions which are intended for a complete spectrum of users. This means that some or many of them will be of no interest to you, and in the pages that follow we shall look at some of the items that fall outside the usual financial applications of spreadsheets.

1 The sheet in Fig. 7.12 shows a table of radians, sines, consines and tangents of angles from 10 degrees to 20 degrees, with seven-figure precision. Underneath is a printout of line 3 after using ◇ ENT on each slot.

Degrees	Radians	Sine	Cos	Tan	
10	0.1745329	0.1736482	0.9848078	0.1763270	
11	0.1919862	0.1908090	0.9816272	0.1943803	
12	0.2094395	0.2079117	0.9781476	0.2125566	
13	0.2268928	0.2249511	0.9743701	0.2308682	
14	0.2443461	0.2419219	0.9702957	0.2493280	
15	0.2617994	0.2588190	0.9659258	0.2679492	
16	0.2792527	0.2756374	0.9612617	0.2867454	
17	0.2967060	0.2923717	0.9563048	0.3057307	
18	0.3141593	0.3090170	0.9510565	0.3249197	
19	0.3316126	0.3255682	0.9455186	0.3443276	
20	0.3490659	0.3420201	0.9396926	0.3639702	(a)
A2+1	rad(A3)	sin(B3)	cos(B3)	tan(B3)	(b)

Figure 7.12 A table (a) of sines, cosines and tangents for a small range of angles. (b) The expressions used.

2 The incrementing of the number of degrees has been carried out by using A2 + 1 as the expression in A3, and this implies that A4 will use A3 + 1 and so on. The values of sine, cos and tan are obtained by the use of PipeDream function. A function is a form of command that acts on a number to produce a result which is usually another number. Note that these angle functions require an angle value in radians, so that the B column is used as the number acted on (the *argument*) rather than the A column.

3 The table has used seven decimal places for display of values other than degrees, which use whole numbers (*integers*) only. This was achieved by setting 7 places of decimals in the Options page. The degrees column was then marked as a block, and ◇ LDP used to specify zero decimal places for that block.

4 The two-dimensional nature of a spreadsheet is illustrated by Fig. 7.13 which shows an application for keeping mark records in a course which is subject to frequent assessment.

Name	Test 1	Test 2	Test 3	Test 4	Test 5	Total	Final %
Potter, D.Z.	22	12	31	34	41	140	48%
Allanby,G.X.	42	27	59	71	65	264	90%
Brightwell,R.Y.	44	24	60	70	66	264	90%
Tipler,B.F.	20	12	26	32	31	121	41%
Totals	67%	63%	68%	65%	73%	67%	67%

Figure 7.13 A spreadsheet used for entering test results.

5 The second line in this example has not been printed; it is used to keep the maximum score for each test, and in the columns from the third line onwards, the test figures are entered. The figures are totalled in column G and converted to percentage in column H.

6 At the bottom of the sheet, percentage averages of all the marks in each text are shown. Since the sheet is used to take a class of up to 20, the actual number must be counted, and this is done in column I by counting the non-blank name entries. The sum of marks down a column is divided by the product of maximum mark and number of tests to give the fraction, and this is multiplied by 100 to obtain the percentage.

7 This printout has been obtained using ◇ PO followed by columns A H (column I omitted) and the row condition !(row = 2|b1 = 0) so that row 2 is not printed, nor any row in which the B column contains a zero. You cannot use a test such as a1 = " " because a text slot cannot be tested, only an expression slot.

Name	Test 1	Test 2	Test 3	Test 4	Test 5	Total	Final %	
Totals line	48	30	65	80	70	293		1
Potter, D.Z.	22	12	31	34	41	140	48%	1
Allanby, G.X.	42	27	59	71	65	264	90%	1
Brightwell, R.Y.	44	24	60	70	66	264	90%	1
Tipler, B.F.	20	12	26	32	31	121	41%	1
	0	0	0	0	0	0	0%	0
	0	0	0	0	0	0	0%	0
	0	0	0	0	0	0	0%	0
	0	0	0	0	0	0	0%	0
	0	0	0	0	0	0	0%	0
	0	0	0	0	0	0	0%	0
	0	0	0	0	0	0	0%	0
	0	0	0	0	0	0	0%	0
	0	0	0	0	0	0	0%	0
	0	0	0	0	0	0	0%	0
	0	0	0	0	0	0	0%	0
	0	0	0	0	0	0	0%	0
	0	0	0	0	0	0	0%	0
	0	0	0	0	0	0	0%	0
	0	0	0	0	0	0	0%	0
Totals	67%	63%	68%	65%	73%	67%	67%	4

Figure 7.14 The printout of the complete sheet shows the totals line and the present/absent column.

8 Figure 7.14 shows the sheet printed with all of its columns and rows, showing the totals row and the present/absent column I. Figure 7.15 shows some of the expressions, omitting those which are simply replicated down or across. Some of the expressions have been taken from a line 22 which was added while the sheet was being extended.

```
sum(B4F4)     G4*100/$G$2              if(B4=0,0,1)
100*sum(B3B20)/($I$22*B$2)
100*sum(B3B20)/($I$22*B$2)
      335%                    2
sum(B21G21)/6
sum(I3I20)
```

Figure 7.15   The expressions of the spreadsheet.

9 The points to note are as follows:

(a) The % sign is obtained by using ◇ LCT. This *trailing character* can be changed in the Options menu. You can use up to four characters in a trailing set, so that trailers like /87, & Co, are possible. Note the use of ◇ LDF for removing these signs.

(b) To find the percentage mark for a candidate, the total (G4) is divided by the maximum total (G2) and multiplied by 100. The G2 amount must be fixed. The layout has specified no decimal places, so that if you did not multiply by 100, the result would be zero.

(c) The marker column, I, uses IF(B4 = 0,0,1). The test must use an expression slot, remember, because a text slot cannot be tested. You might, of course, have declared all the A slots as expression slots, entered '' '' for a blank name, and put in the actual names using quotes.

(d) The calcuation of overall percentage for all the candidates in one test (last row in columns b to F) uses the total number of candidates in I22. This number multiplied by the maximum score for that test (row 2 fixed) gives the amount which is divided into the actual test total, and hence the percentage.

(*e*) The overall percentage has been taken the simple way, by summing the percentages for the five tests and the sum, and then dividing by 6. It would have been quicker to ignore the sum and use B to F, dividing by 5.

10 The planning of a spreadsheet is important, but it is even more important to check the results carefully. A mistake in an expression can result in a sheet that looks very convincing but which is complete nonsense. Tests, in particular, need to be looked at very carefully, remembering that only expression slots can be tested.

■ SECTION 53

Other functions

To illustrate each one of the functions that can be used in expression slots would take more space than has already been used by this book. In this Section, then, we shall review very briefly some of the items that can be used.

1 Dates are often useful. A date can be entered into an expression slot as, for example, 02.03.1988, using two digits each for day and month, and four for year. You can then extract the day, month of year number by using expressions such as DAY(A1), MONTH(A1), YEAR(A1). A date can be changed in the form: A1 + 26 to give a new date, so that it is possible to have a column that contains automatically incremented dates, like a diary format.

2 You can specify more than one slot, and also restricted ranges, in a list. A list takes a form such as (A1 A7,C4,M2 M5), which would specify the use of A1 to A7, C4, then M2 to M5 respectively. The functions that make use of such a list are CHOOSE, COUNT, MAX, MIN, SUM.

   (a) CHOOSE (B2,7,11,23,31,56) would use the value in B2 to choose from the list of numbers that follows, starting at the first number following B2. If B2 contained 3, then the number 23 would be used. If the list consisted entirely of slot references, then what appears is the number or string in the selected slot. This allows a value that you enter in a slot to pick a value in another slot. If the number that is used to choose is impossible (pick the 15th in a list of 5) then the warning *Too few arguments* will appear in the CHOOSE slot.

   (b) COUNT (A1, E1,B5,C7 C9) will give the number of slots that are in use as expression slots. This can be useful if you need a total that excluded non-entered slots.

   (c) MAX(A1 E1,B4,C2 C6) will give the highest number that occurs in this list of slots, and MIN(list) will give the smallest number found in the list.

   (d) SUM (B2 B5, D3, A12 F12) will give the sum total of all the numbers in the list of slots

3 The LOOKUP function can be remarkably useful in dealing
with items that do not follow a mathematical relationship.
The command:

   LOOKUP(3,A1   A10,B1   B10)

will find where the number 3 is in the set of slots from A1 to
A10, and give the number that is in the corresponding position in the range B1 to B10. The ranges must either be equal,
or range B should be greater.

   If, for example the number 3 were located in A6, then the
number printed would be the number in B6. The first number
can be a date or a slot reference. The manual states that a
string can be used, but it was not acceptable on my Z88.
The use of a slot reference means, however, that you could
type *man* into a slot and get the translation *homme* in
another if your spreadsheet contained tables of English and
French words.

   Your tables might, on the other hand contain dates and
values of transactions – the LOOKUP function allows you to
find the item you are looking for in a table that has not been
sorted.

4 Certain values such as dates, page numbers and slot values
can be transferred to a word-processed document. We have
used the page number already (headers and footers, Section
44), and a date is placed in with @D@. You can also place a
slot value in with, for example, @F7@. This has to be used
carefully, as it can upset the formatting of words on a line,
unless the slot reference is in a line of its own. To force the
word-processor formatting to make room, use something like
@F7@@@@, in which the five @ characters make space
for a five-digit number or five letter word.

Part 8
Database Use

The use of PipeDream as a database will be covered fairly briefly here, because so many of the database actions have been covered already in connection with other topics. In addition, the selections that can be made of column and row in the Spreadsheet application of PipeDream amount to some database capability.

The purpose of a Database is to store a set of related items in such a way that access is made easy. In a telephone number database, for example, you could type a name or part of a name and in a fraction of a second get a telephone number which you could then dial for the next hour in the hope of contacting someone.

Because the very large databases kept mainly by large organis-ations (excluding government departments) are thought to be a threat to privacy, the Data Protection Act is now in force. This has been drafted with the same Parliamentary care and foresight as the laws that make it legal to buy sex magazines on Sunday but not Bibles.

The result is that if you, on a Z88, dare to keep a database that contains anything more than the names, addresses and telephone numbers of friends you are liable to register under this Act, providing the government with a useful licence fee. The situation that is arising from this resembles the law as applied to cassette tapes and videos – you are allowed to possess cassette recorders and video recorders but most people break the law when using them.

Until the Act is amended, then, to take account of the types of computers that are around these days, you are obliged to register if you keep personal details of anyone for anything other than a friendly relationship (you may keep your Christmas card list as long as no business friends, butcher, baker or candlestick-maker, are included). You may keep a mailing list for business use if the list consists only of names and addresses (no categories like type of work, age group and so on allowed) and if all the names on your list assent to being on the list. There are also limited exemptions if you use your computer to keep records of an unincorporated club.

If you think that your use of data may be exempt, you should take a look at Guideline 6, Data Protection Act 1984 (The Exemptions) from the Office of the Data Protection Registrar, Springfield House, Water Lane, Wilmslow, Cheshire SK9 5AX. The telephone number is (0625) 535777 (and this is the type of data you can keep without fear of transgressing the Act). There are eight booklets of Guidelines, all of which are free of charge. If you want to keep really confidential data on employees, business contacts or others, keep it on a card file, to which the Act does not apply. It is apparently thought that keeping information on a computer file is more more invasive of privacy than keeping it on a card file, and this includes Filofax. Cheer up, they might have made you carry a red flag each time you used your Z88.

Planning

The first step in using the Database actions of PipeDream is to decide in what form you want to store the data. This, in turn, is closely tied up with what use you intend to make of it.

If at some future date, you intend to find out how many lawyers in East Anglia specialise in interpretation of the Data Protection Act, then your data list must include lawyers, geographical locations, and specialities. If you want to know if your lawyers have technical qualifications, then you need another entry for this.

Each item that has to be entered goes into a separate *field*, its own slot in the database. The whole database will usually be saved as a file, and will have to be loaded in again to be used, unlike the databases used with larger machines. The exception to this is if you use a list file you can search all the files in a list.

1 Your plan must therefore start with the number of fields and their widths. For a name and telephone number database, for example, you might use surnames of up to fifteen characters and telephone numbers which could be of up to twelve characters.

2 Such a list as it is entered might look as in Fig.8.1. The widths of the slots have been made to fit the field sizes, and the names are in random order. You may find it useful to use the options page (⬦ O) to turn off wordwrap.

```
Simpkins      09-414-212
Clotberg      08-112-706
Abler         09-223-621
Bakerman      08-221-806
Zottler       09-611-202
```

Figure 8.1 A list of imaginary names and telephone numbers as entered.

3 You can search the list by using ◇ BSE. Note that the list does *not* have to marked as a block in order to allow searching. Remember that searching allows you to use the wildcards ⌃ ? and ⌃ # , and you can also speed up searching by stipulating the column to search. If you are searching for a name that starts Abl, for example, you can use Abl⌃ # and the names column A only.

4 To sort the list into order, you first have to mark the items as a block. Once marked, you can use ◇ BSO, and specify which column to use for sorting. For a list that includes names, this will usually be on the name column. Figure 8.2 shows the sorted list – note that the list remains sorted, it is not simply displayed or printed as a sorted list leaving the original as it was.

```
Abler          09-223-621
Bakerman       08-221-806
Clotberg       08-112-706
Simpkins       09-414-212
Zottler        09-611-202
```

Figure 8.2   The list sorted by name.

Data forms

The data types that you can use in Database slots are the same as the data types you can use in other applications of PipeDream, text or expression types. Unless you have decreed otherwise, each slot will start as a text slot, but if you want to enter numerical data you have the choice of using a text slot or an expression slot.

Actions like searching and sorting make no distinction about type of slot, but if you enter numerical data into a text slot you will have to arrange·the data for yourself – it will not be automatically have decimal points lined up, for example.

If your data includes items like money sums, examination marks and anything that might include decimal points and/or marks like pound signs and percentages, then an expression slot is probably more appropriate.

1 Figure 8.3 shows the list of names, with the names in text slots and amounts of money in expression slots. This list has been sorted by order of money amount, in reverse order so that the largest money sum appears at the top of the list.

```
Simpkins        £65.20
Clotberg        £51.40
Zottler         £33.70
Bakerman        £22.70
Abler           £22.60
```

Figure 8.3   A list sorted by money amounts, largest amounts first.

2 Figure 8.4 shows dates added to the list. Dates should always be put into an expression slot, because this allows them to be sorted in strict time order, something that is not done if the date is written as a string. The dates can be typed as 01.04.1987 or in the shorter form like 2.6.1987; the form seen on the screen will be 4.11.1984 or suchlike.

```
Zottler              £33.70     6.9.1979
Clotberg             £51.40     4.6.1981
Simpkins             £65.20     1.5.1982
Abler                £22.60    10.4.1985
Bakerman             £22.70    12.12.1986
```

Figure 8.4 Dates added to the list, and sorted by date.

```
Clotberg             £51.40     4.6.1981       44.00%
Bakerman             £22.70    12.12.1986       56.00%
Zottler              £33.70     6.9.1979       58.00%
Abler                £22.60    10.4.1985       62.00%
Simpkins             £65.20     1.5.1982       68.00%
```

Figure 8.5 Percentages added to the list.

3 Percentage figures are illustrated in Fig.8.5. These have, as before, been typed into an expression slot so that the ◇ LCT command can be used to put in the % sign.

4 Remember that when you prepare a database you can use the same techniques as you use for a spreadsheet, marking the slots in the first line that will be used as expression slots, along with any leading or trailing characters, and then replicating throughout the rest of the document. This saves a considerable amount of time in the use of ◇ X for each expression slot, and also avoids the need to remember which slots are expression slots.

5 You can, however, use ◇ ENT to convert slots if you have entered them in the wrong way. Figure 8.6 shows what happens if dates are entered into slot C without converting this into an expression slot, and then sorting. The sort is by the day figure rather than by the full date. To remedy this, you could mark this column as a block, and use ◇ ENT, then remove the mark with ◇ Q.

```
Clotberg             £51.40 04.06.1981         44.00%
Zottler              £33.70 06.09.79           58.00%
Abler                £22.60 10.04.85           62.00%
Bakerman             £22.70 12.12.86           56.00%
```

Figure 8.6 How dates appear when placed in to a text slot – note how the date is placed at the left-hand side of the slot.

123

SECTION 56

Selective printing

You can select items for printing even if the selection uses strings in text slots. You can, for example, use <> PO to print, and in the Row choice specify Yes A1 = "Abler" to obtain only the data line for this one entry.

Comparisons of numbers, strings or dates can use > meaning greater than, < meaning less than, and <> meaning not equal to. The < and > signs can also be used along with the equality sign to mean < = less than or equal to, and > = greater than or equal to.

1 In the example used previously, we can command a printout with <> PO and then specify in the Row selection:

   YES b1 > 30

   so that only the data for those whose money column is greater than £30 will be printed out.

2 We could just as easily use b1 < = 30 to print all the data for those whose money amount was equal to £30 or less than £30. We are not confined, either to printing out all data; it would be just as easy to print the name column only, using the same selection criterion for rows.

3 Slot references that are used in expressions for printing are updated just like slot references in Spreadsheet use – we are, after all, still using the same program.

4 Conditions can be combined. If, for example, you use:

   YES b1 < 30 & CI > 1.1.1981

   you will get the data for those who have a money amount less than £30 and also a date following 1.1.1981. Note that you have to specify the date in full – just 1981 will not do.

5 The symbols that are used are:

   & to mean AND (Print only if two or more conditions are satisfied at the same time).

   | to mean OR (print if one or more conditions are true)

   ! to mean NOT (used to invert the sense of a condition)

The NOT statement can be useful to get the rest of the list after the use of a condition has produced one list. It is also used in formulating conditions like !(row = 2) (not row 2, so use every other row) as an alternative to ROW <> 2.

6 The only problem that arises is identifying a text slot that contains nothing, since a test like: a1 <> " " does not work. You need in such cases to devise some other form of test.

Logic equivalents

Tests that make use of the logic commands can always be formulated in more than one way, and in most cases, one form of logic will be easier then another. Unless you have had some experience with logic statements in a programming language like BASIC, or with programs like dBASE II, you will find these tests confusing at first.

The most important point to remember at this stage is that there is a general rule that links the alternative forms of logic. It can be put in the forms:

NOT(A) OR NOT(B) = NOT (A AND B)   or   !A|!B = !(A&B)

in which the second form uses the symbols of PipeDream.

Before we look at how this rule is implemented, consider one very common logic fault which often baffles users of databases and spreadsheets.

1 Suppose (not referring to any previous example) you want to print out the lines in which C1 is less then 30, D1 is not "London" and E1 is not between 50 and 60. You might be tempted to write the line:

C1 < 30 & D1 <> "London" & E1 < 50 & E1 > 60

which is not likely to be useful. The & sign, logical AND, means that conditions must be *simultaneously* satisfied. It is unlikely that E1 will contain a number that is both less than 50 and greater than 60.

2 The fault is the use of & between the last two parts of the condition, which ought to read:

C1 < 30 & D1 <> "London" & (E1 < 50 | E1 > 60)

in which the last part, (E1 < 50 | E1 > 60) will be true if either condition is true.

3 Now suppose that you want to use the condition in which the sense is:

NOT(A1 = "London") OR NOT(B1 > 50)

so that you proceed if A1 is not "London" or if B1 is not more than 50. By using the rule above, you can convert this to:

NOT(A1 = "London" & B1 > 50)

which is shorter.

4 Note how brackets can be used in logical statements to convey the same sense of priority as they do in mathematical expressions. Whatever is held inside a bracket is one unit whose value is worked out before anything else.

5 When you are designing a database, provide a field for each possible piece of information. Even if you do not need the extra data at the moment, it is highly likely that you will later. You can select and print only the data that you need.

Part 9
Data Printing and Transfer

Part 6 has already dealt with some of the requirements for using a serial printer, and these points will not be repeated here. The electrical connections must be correct, and the computer and printer set up so that the baud rate, use of parity and Xon/Xoff are identical.

Parity is a method of checking for errors. The normal parity system depends on the fact that the standard ASCII code for printable characters uses only seven out of a set of eight electrical signals, and the eighth signal can be used to identify a mistake.

The signalling is on the basis of an odd or even signal count. Each signal of the set is either present or absent, and the eighth signal can be used to make the total number of signals present either even or odd. This is why parity can be described as either even or odd.

Many computer printers make use of the eighth signal to give another set of characters, and many computers can take advantage of this. For that reason, it is often undesirable to make use of parity in serial signals for printers.

The Xon/Xoff system is one method of allowing the printer to control the rate at which the computer sends data. The computer can send data much faster than any printer can use it, so that some system is needed to control the rate.

One method is to keep the baud rate so low that it is lower than the rate of printing. Another is to equip the printer with a large (*buffer*) memory, so that all the data can be transferred quickly for the printer to work on slowly.

The more usual system, however, is some form of *handshaking* in which signals are passed between the computer and the printer to indicate when more data is to be sent, or when data flow must be interrupted.

When the electrical connections permit, these extra handshaking signals can be passed over separate wires, allowing the signals to be independently transmitted. The alternative is to use the normal signal connections to send special codes. These are the Xon and Xoff codes, meaning transmit on and transmit off.

For most applications, you will not need this latter method, so that it can be disabled.

■ SECTION 58

Printer control

The control of the printer, whether the link to the printer is serial or parallel, is carried out by sending code signals to the printer. The signals consist of either number codes less than 32 (32 is the ASCII code for the space) or codes that are preceded by 27 (often shown as ESC in printer documentation).

You cannot send these codes out as a normal part of PipeDream or Diary, but they can be programmed by using PrinterEd. Precisely what you can do using PrinterEd depends on the type of printer that you use, and in this respect a dot-matrix printer is very much more versatile than a daisywheel. The examples that follow have been produced using an Epson RX-80 dot-matrix printer. The standard setup of PrinterEd is for the later FX type, but the differences are minor.

Note that any changes that you make with the PrinterEd have no effect until you have used the ⬦ FU command – see Section 62.

1. Use INDEX to locate PrinterEd, or press ☐ E. The menu for PrinterEd consists of two pages, and the first that appears is concerned with the appearance of the highlighting effects.

2. This first menu lists the highlight numbers 1 to 8 down the left-hand side, followed by lists of codes for turning the effect on, and turning it off. There is also a column that will determine if the highlight effect is turned off automatically at a 'carriage return', the ENTER key code.

3. As the machine comes to you, several of these codes will already be filled in. Underline, for example, is given as 27,45,1 to turn on and 27,45,0 to turn off. This would not suit a Juki daisywheel printer which needs 27,69 to turn on underline and 27,82 to turn it off.

4. Because these codes differ from one printer to another (though most dot-matrix printers adhere fairly closely to the Epson codes) you can find that a document which looks fine on the screen and prints perfectly on an Epson dot-matrix printer will give very odd output on another type of printer.

5 You need, therefore, if you are using another printer, to go over these codes very carefully to be sure that they correspond to what you want. Note that you do not need to modify any of your documents, only the PrinterEd lines.

6 Most of the effects have one code to turn on and another to turn off. If in doubt, arrange for the effect to turn off with CR, because this can avoid printing pages of unsuitable text.

Ext. sequence and user defined text

PrinterEd allows you to fill in values for two highlight codes that are not present in the machine when you receive it. The Ext. sequence code appears to be intended to allow you to print one special character, such as the German umlaut, and the User defined code allows some print style other then bold or italic to be used.

For the Epson printer, the use of wide print is the most common user-defined choice, and this can be added; or you can make a choice suited to your printer.

The special characters that you add depend on what is available from your printer, particularly if this is a daisywheel type. Do not include here such characters as the £ sign which are on the Z88 keyboard, because there are better methods of obtaining such characters.

1 To print a German umlaut with an Epson, you have to switch to the German character set with 27,82, 2 print a suitable character such as 93, then switch back to the English character set with 27,82,3.

2 This can be done in two ways. One is to type in the Ext. sequence line the set:

   27,82,2,93,27,82,3

which will change to the German set, print the U umlaut, and then switch back. No second ◇ PX code will be needed.

3 The alternative is to put 27,82,2 as the ON set and 27,82,3 as the off, so that ◇ PX will switch to the German character set and ◇ PX repeated will switch off. This is illustrated in Fig.9.1.

```
We now switch to German characters.
using [ \ ] which appear as
Ä ö Ü  in this set          -
```

Figure 9.1 Obtaining the German umlaut characters on the Epson printer.

4 The User defined text that you can use very much depends on your printer, and with a daisywheel printer there might not be anything useful available, since changing type on a daisywheel is done by changing printwheels rather then by software.

5 Figure 9.2 shows the wide character set of the Epson RX80 in use, after programming as the User-defined type of the Z88. The switch on code is 14 and the switch off is 20. (Note: code 27 is not used in this case.)

```
This uses user defined  characters
of the Epson printer.
```

Figure 9.2 The wide character set of the RX-80 used as the user-defined type.

■ SECTION 60

Printer initialisation

Each time a printer is used, the Z88 system allows for codes, called initialisation codes, to be sent. These are arranged on Page 2 of PrinterEd, obtained by using SHIFT and the down-cursor.

Also in this page are useful options about line feed and end of page codes, and provision for microspacing which is available on some printer types.

1 The first item in this page is labelled as Printer on. The code that is supplied is 27,64, which is the printer initialisation code of the Epson, cancelling any other effects. You will probably want to keep this if you use an Epson, but note that other printers can differ – for example, the Juki daisy-wheel uses 27,26,73.

2 You may wish to add codes to the 'Printer on' set. The Epson uses 27,56 to disable the paper-out switch, so that this code should be added if you are working with single sheets.

3 You may also want to carry out most of your printing with a typeface other than the normal ten pitch one. Most of the illustrations in this book were printed with the Epson set to Elite twelve pitch, for which the code is 27,77.

4 The Alternate font option in Page 1 of PrinterEd may have to be changed if you opt for another type font as standard. If, for example, you set up to use Elite at the start of printing, you might want to use Pica (10 pitch) for other purposes. This can be done by using the codes 27,80 to switch on and 27,77 to switch off in the Alternate font option. Figure 9.3 illustrates this use.

```
The normal elite font can be replaced by pica for
this purpose. The pica is larger and fainter
```

Figure 9.3 Using standard Elite and alternative Pica type.

5 You can put in printer-off code if you wish, though this is seldom needed. No code is put into this heading as standard.

6 You can use the 'End of page' option to decide how your printer behaves after printing a document. If you are using a lot of short printouts, as in this book, retaining the standard code of 12 results in the printer reeling out a page of paper for each short printout. Changing the 12 to 10 causes only a line feed after a print out.

7 The 'Allow line feed' option allows the printer end of line codes to be tailored to your printer. If you find that all your printing is double-spaced when you have specified single-spacing, cancel this option by typing N.

8 The HMI microspacing options are of specialist interest only.

Translation of characters

The PrinterEd system also allows for translations of code, so that the code which is used for a character on screen is not the same as the code sent to the printer.

The built-in translation is for the pound sign, making PipeDream one of the few pieces of software which can use a £ sign on screen and also print the symbol without elaborate work.

The code for £ used within the computer is 163, and the code for the Epson involves changing to the English character set, printing the # sign, then back to the US (or whatever) character set. If you use the machine always with the English character set, you can use the # sign as the translation with no change of character sets.

1 The pound translation is given as 163 to 27, 82, 3, 35, 27, 82, 0 which follows the sequence given above. If your initialisation process uses a switch to the English character set (all right if you don't need the # character), then only the 35 (ASCII code for #) is needed of this set.

2 Another translation which is sometimes useful is the carat sign ʌ into an up-arrow. The up-arrow on the Epson RX80 is one of a set of graphics symbols that requires switching on with 27,"m", 4 and off afterwards with 27,"m",0. The code for the up-arrow is 155, and so the complete translation is from 94 "ʌ" to 27, "m",4,94,27,"m",0. The effect is illustrated in Fig.9.4.

The carat can be replaced by the up-arrow, giving effects such as 10↑6 and ↑↑↑↑↑↑

Figure 9.4 The carat sign replaced by an up-arrow.

3 Other translations that you might want are the mathematical multiply and divide signs to replace ∗ and /. For some purposes, you might like to replace the dollar and ~ signs by the + / − and musical note signs. These can be programmed as:

Character "∗"
Changes to 27,"m",4,157,27,"m",0
Character "/"
Changes to 27,"m"4,158,27,"m",0
Character "$"
Changes to 27,"m",4,159,27,"m",0
Character "~"
Changes to 27,"m",4,149,27,"m",0

The effects are demonstrated in Fig.9.5.

```
We can now write 34 × 42 and 15 ÷ 12
The dimension is 22.4 ± 0.05 mm
Look for the ♪♪♪ on the screen.
```

Figure 9.5 A few other translations in use.

Fixing the changes

The changes that are made with PrinterEd are not fixed in the system until the ◇ FU command has been executed. When you press this key combination, you will see the cursor disappear, and you should not enter anything until it reappears.

When the cursor reappears, the printer changes have been made, and all the effects that have been programmed in the latter pages will be active.

1 You might want to have your original printer driver back at some stage. This is done by pressing ◇ FNEW at any time, and you do not need to press ◇ FU to bring the driver into action.

2 Recalling a changed printer code set is not possible unless you have recorded it, by using ◇ FS and giving a file name. You should always ensure that you have a file copy of any printer driver set of your own before making alterations.

3 You should also file your changed set of codes, so that you can thereafter switch easily between sets. This can save a great deal of effort if you have conflicting requirements for printing.

4 Once you make a set of altered printer codes active with ◇ FU this set will remain in use until you make more changes by hand or load in a different set and use ◇ FU again, or use ◇ FNEW.

5 If you have made extensive changes with PrinterEd because you are using a different type of printer, you may like to change the name that appears in PrinterEd, which is set at Epson as standard. You alter this by typing ◇ FC and typing the new name (Juki, Star, HewPack or whatever).

■ SECTION 63

Transfers of data

Unless you have considerably expanded the memory of your Z88, you will frequently come up against memory limitations. Even with the expanded memory, you cannot keep filing work for long before running out of memory. Unless you have a Z88 disk system, you will be forced either to abandon work or transfer it to another machine.

All files created in the Z88 can be transferred. This does not mean that they can be used by any other machine, only that they can be stored on the disks of another machine.

Ordinary word processed text with no highlight codes can be transferred and used by a word processor on another machine, but Diary and Spreadsheet entries are less likely to be usable, and Database actions are unlikely to transfer easily to other programs.

The main reason for transfer, then, is storage, along with the possibility of using text with WordStar, Word or other word processing programs on the other machine.

Cambridge Computers have announced cables and software for transfers between the PC type of machine and the BBC computer. In this book, I shall deal with transfer to and from the Amstrad PC1541, because such transfers are very simple and require no special software, and little hardware other than a standard serial printer cable.

This should not be taken to imply that you can connect any PC type of machine easily, and unless you are prepared to take some time to experiment you should take the pages that follow as a guide that applies to the Amstrad PC1541 only, though the advice is probably relevant to most compatible machines.

If you have any doubts, then rely on the Cambridge Computers package, using the following pages only as a guide to what can be done rather than as a description of how to carry out the transfers. The software of the Cambridge Computers package also allows conversions of data so that you can, for example, transfer Wordstar or Lotus 1–2–3 files to PipeDream and use them directly.

Z88 to Amstrad PC 1512 – hardware

The hardware for data transfer consists of a suitable cable to connect the nine-pin socket on the Z88 to the 25-pin plug on the PC1512. Since only six pins are actually used, this is not quite such a problem as it seems.

1 If you can make up cables for yourself, or can have them made up for you, the connections are as shown in Fig.9.6. I used standard telephone extension cable, with six cores and earth, and made intermediate connection through a 25-pin plug so that I could use the same cable for my printer.

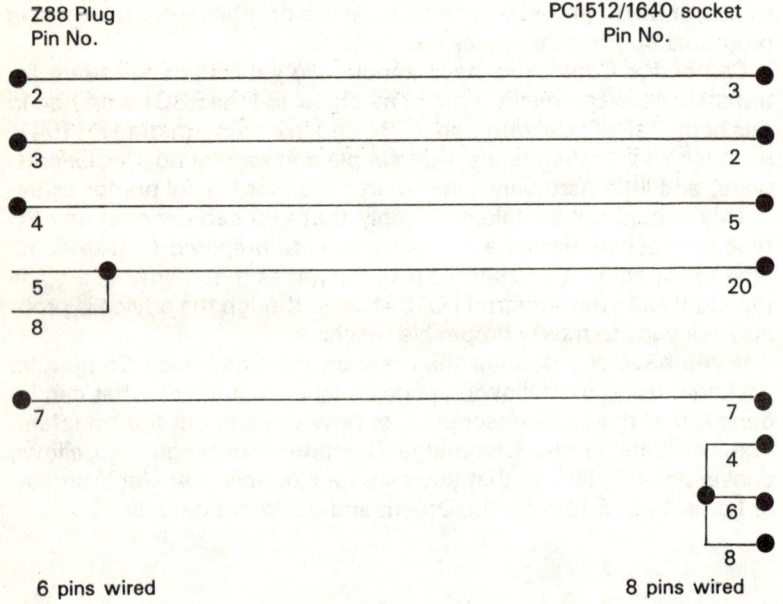

Z88 Plug
Pin No.

PC1512/1640 socket
Pin No.

6 pins wired   8 pins wired

Note: This connection is almost identical to a serial printer connection, except that printer cable uses a 25-way plug rather than a socket.

Figure 9.6 Connections for a serial transfer cable, Z88 to Amstrad PC.

2 If you have a Z88 serial printer cable, you might be able to achieve transfer by coupling the printer plug to the PC with a socket-to-socket cable, sometimes known as a *gender-changer* (not a new type of pop-star).

3 The essential point is that the connection to pin 2 at the Z88 must go to pin 3 at the PC, and pin 2 at the PC end must go to pin 3 at the Z88. If this is not correct, transfer will never be possible, because these are the signal connections.

4 The other connections are needed for hand-shaking, and if you find that only one-way transfer is possible, then a fault exists in one of these lines, or in the way that pins are connected together at either end. The connection of pins 5 and 8 at the Z88 end, for example, is needed if you want to transfer data into the Z88 from the PC.

5 Whenever you have proved that a cable works, make sure that it is securely clamped. Some plugs and sockets are troublesome, and if the surrounding shells are attached, the plugs cannot be fitted. The only remedy is to use a different make of plug or socket.

6 Serial cables can be fairly long, but unless you have a special need for long cable, restrict lengths to five metres maximum. The longer the cable, the more difficulty you will have with interference and with corrupted text, particularly if you use fast baud rates.

Z88 to PC software

The software for a 88 to PC transfer is minimal, and consists of using the DOS-Plus operating system of the PC1512. The later PC1640 can use the COPY command of MS–DOS for the same purpose – for details see the PC1640 manual. The instructions in the book relate to the PC1512 only. There is more than one method, however, of transmitting files as far as the Z88 is concerned.

1 At the PC, make sure that the baud rate and other protocols are set correctly. Figure 9.7 shows settings for 2400 baud, a useful rate, and how this can be set as a standard for each time the transfer is to be done.

Temporary change:

PC1512 using DOS-Plus:
1. Make sure that the DOS-Plus disk is in the drive.
2. Type MODE COM1:2400,N,8,1.
3. Press RETURN.

PC1640 using MS-DOS:
1. Make sure that the MS-DOS disk is in the drive.
2. Type MODE COM1:2400,N,8,1.
3. Press RETURN.

Permanent change:
1. Make sure that the disk in the drive contains the NVR.EXE program.
2. Type NVR and press RETURN.
3. When menu appears, use the down-arrow key of the PC to select the line that reads: Standard RS232 Parameters. Press RETURN.
4. Select Transmission rate 2400, Parity None, Number of data bits 8, Number of stop bits 1. Flow control OFF.
5. Move cursor to EXIT, press RETURN.
6. Select 'Save these alterations to RAM, press RETURN.
7. The settings will be ready for use each time the machine is switched on.

Figure 9.7 Setting the PC to 2400 baud and other necessary protocols.

2 With the protocols set up, and the DOS-Plus disk in the drive, type PIP. Wait until an asterisk appears on screen, and then remove the DOS-Plus disk and insert a formatted blank disk. If you have two drives (or a hard disk) you can keep the DOS-Plus disk in place and specify B: or C: for the data at a later stage.

3 At the Z88, make sure that the file you want to send is in RAM memory, not just a PipeDream suspended file. You need to know the filename of the file you want to transfer.

4 AT the PC, type A:filename = AUX[e] if you are using one drive, or use B:filename or C:filename if you have more than one drive. The asterisk should disappear when you press RETURN.

5 At the Z88, use □ X or INDEX to get to the Import/Export menu. Press S for 'send file', then ENTER. Type the filename of the file in the ROM that you want to send.

6 Press ENTER on the Z88 to send the file, and watch the lines of the file appear on the PC's screen – only one line is shown on the screen.

7 When the file has transferred leave Import/Export and enter Terminal with □ V. On the blank Terminal screen, type ◇ Z. You should hear the disk drive of the PC start, recording your data.

8 Leave Terminal with SHIFT ENTER. You can now inspect your data on the PC by pressing RETURN to leave the PIP program, and using TYPE filename to inspect the data.

9 If you want to send more data, do not press RETURN at the PC, but type another filename = AUX:[e] instruction.

NOTE: If you have the Ability program which is now bundled with the PC1512, you can transfer data using the COMMUNI-CATIONS facility of Ability.

143

An alternative – Z88 to PC1512

An alternative method makes use of the Terminal only, bypassing Import/Export. The disadvantage is that it needs slightly more preparation on the PipeDream file.

1 Prepare the PC in the way described in the previous Section, using PIP and the B:filename = AUX[e] type of instruction.

2 At the Z88, load the file into PipeDream and edit it so that it starts with a single line containing # V. This makes the file go to the Terminal program. End the file with the characters |Z.

3 Now make use of the Filer program by pressing ☐ F or by using the Index. Press ◇ EX, which is the command for *execute file* as applied to a file that contains commands. You are asked to supply a filename.

4 When you press ENTER, the # V at the start of the file is interpreted as ☐ V, so that the Terminal program is entered. The contents of the file are then sent to the Terminal, and so to the PC over the serial link. At the end of the file |Z is interpreted as ◇ Z, sending the end-of-file code which will place the file on disk and switch the PC machine back to awaiting another file-transfer command.

5 This scheme can be upset if your file contains the characters # and |, and lines starting with a full-stop can also cause problems. If this is so, then add into your file the command:

  J.

as the second line (the dot as the first character in the line, and with nothing else in that line), and remove the |Z at the end. You will then have to end the file manually by pressing the ◇ Z keys.

6 It ought to be possible to send a file direct from PipeDream by using ◇ FS and specifying :COM.1/filename when prompted for a filename. Though I was able to use this form with ◇ FL to load into PipeDream (see later), I could not save files in this convenient way.

■ SECTION 67

PC to Z88

Transferring data from the PC into the Z88 is possibly by three methods, one of which is particularly convenient for documents. The steps that are taken at the PC end are similar to those used for transfer in the opposite direction, and demand the use of DOS-Plus on the PC1512, or the COPY command on the PC1640. The instructions that follow are for use on the PC1512.

The first method will load data into PipeDream directly. This data must, however, be suitable for PipeDream in the sense that only plain ASCII code may be used.

Files from Wordstar and many other word-processors that are used on the PC contain codes in the range 128–255 which are used to mark the end of a word. Such files cannot be transferred satisfactorily.

These word-processors, have the facility to generate a *non-document* or *plain ASCII* file quickly and easily, and such a file can be sent to PipeDream.

The following pages assume that you have set up both the PC and the Z88 to the same baud rate and transfer method – preferably 2400 baud and Xon/Xoff not used.

1 At the PC end, load PIP and when the asterisk appears you can change disks if you are using a single-disk system. Type AUX: = filename, in which you can use filenames such as A:Chap1.txt or B:doc.tex, including a drive letter, name and extension letter for your ASCII file.

2 At the Z88, start a PipeDream document, and press ◇ FL to load in a file. When you are prompted for a filename, type:

   :COM.0/filename

using a filename which can be used on the Z88. Filenames such as A:Chap1.text *cannot* be used on the Z88 because of the use of the colon.

3 When you press ENTER on the Z88 and then RETURN on the PC, the file will be transferred. There is no visible sign of what is happening in the sense of seeing the characters of the file being loaded. You know that transfer is complete when the asterisk mark of PIP shows again on the PC screen. You may need to use the CTRL-Z keys on the PC to end the transmission.

4 You may find that you need to switch the Z88 off and on again to see the file in PipeDream, and you may also find that the width of your text has been reduced to one slot. This is simply a matter of editing (◇ H will restore the text width), and the problem is caused by codes in the transmitted text if you have not specified a plain ASCII text.

5 If a file is too long for PipeDream, the transfer will stop with *Memory full* # message.

Import/Export use

The use of the Import/Export program can often be better for file transfers from the PC to the Z88. In particular, you can transfer WordStar and similar files directly without needing to make a plain ASCII copy, because the action of Import/Export will change the file (filter it) on its way.

The steps that are needed at the PC end of the transfer are exactly the same as in Section 65, using PIP on the PC1512 or COPY on the PC1640.

1 At the Z88, switch to Import/Export by using ☐ X. Now press R to receive a file, and press ENTER.

2 You will be asked to name the file. You can use any valid Z88 filename; do not use PC names with drive letters such as A: or B:.

3 Press ENTER on the Z88 after specifying the filename and the press RETURN at the PC to start the transmission. While the file is being transmitted, you will see line numbers appear on the Z88 screen.

4 You may find that the Z88 lines are very short when the file is read into PipeDream, but this can be altered by reformatting.

5 If the file is too long to load, it will be abandoned, and nothing will be loaded.

6 You may need to use CTRL-Z at the PC to end the transmission, but this is usually unnecessary.

Terminal use – files

There is a third method of file transfer which uses Terminal, and has the advantage that the characters of the file appear on the Z88 screen as the file is transferred.

This, however, can cause problems because of the slow speed at which characters are placed on the screen. At a baud rate of 2400, with the simple type of transfer system described here, some characters may be omitted from a file when this method is used. This may not be a problem if the approved Cambridge Computers cable and software is used.

The procedure at the PC end of the transfer is as before.

1 At the Z88, enter Terminal with ☐ V. This gives a blank screen, on which nothing normally appears when you type. Type the command ☐ + S, which directs everything entered into the terminal into a file.

2 Now press the RETURN key on the PC. You should see the characters of the transferred file appear on the screen, because Terminal shows received characters, though not transmitted characters.

3 At the end of the transmission, type on the Z88 keyboard ☐ – S to mark the end of the file. The transmitted characters now exist as a file called :RAM. – /S.sgn. This is not in the normal RAM.0 memory, so when you want to load the file into PipeDream you have to specify this special filename.

4 If the transmitted file has been too long, the file :RAM.0/S.sgn will not exist.

■ SECTION 70

Other Terminal use

The Terminal program can be used to allow one machine to control the other when the machines are connected by a serial cable. You can, for example, use the Z88 keyboard to enter data into the PC as if it had been typed on the keyboard of the PC.

You can also use the PC keyboard to type data which will appear on the Z88 screen. In the simplest Terminal system, you cannot use both directions at once, and in this book, we shall deal only with the simplest method because the topic is not one that many users will need.

1 **To transmit from the Z88 to the PC, use the PIP command of DOS-Plus on the PC1512, and when the asterisk shows, type:**

   CON: = AUX: (Press RETURN)

to transfer everything that appears at the serial link to the PC screen.

2 **Note that this does *not* imply anything other then screen appearance. This method is intended only to allow messages to be passed between operators, not to create disk files. If you want what you type to be transferred to a disk file as well as to the screen, type:**

   B:file.txt = aux:[e]

– assuming that you want the file on drive B, and provide a suitable filename.

3 **At the Z88 enter Terminal with □ V and type whatever you want to send. One major problem is that you do not see on screen what you are typing.**

4 **Your text will not take a new line unless you type ◇ J. At the end of each line, therefore, you should type ENTER ◇ J to ensure that the text at the PC end will be readable.**

5 **The transmission is ended by typing ◇ Z.**

6 To transmit from the PC, use PIP (PC1512) and when the asterisk appears, type:

AUX: = CON: (Press RETURN).

7 At the Z88, enter Terminal with □ V. As characters are typed on the PC keyboard they will also appear on the Z88 screen. The transmission is ended by typing CTRL-Z.

8 If you have typed at the Z88 after entering Terminal □ + S, the characters will be placed in a file called :RAM. – /S.sgn. If you use □ P, the characters will be sent to a printer (not a serial printer, however, since the serial link is being used). These effects have to be turned off with □ – S and □ – P.

SECTION 71

Filer

All of the main programs of the Z88 make use of files, and we have in the course of this book made use of the more common commands of the Filer that relate to the naming, saving and loading of files.

The Z88 allows for a file system to be used that resembles the method used in the PC for hard disks. This system allows files to be grouped into directories so that files of the same name could be stored in different directory groups, using filenames such as BOOK1/Chap1. In this scheme, the directory name comes first, then the name of the file. Several layers of directories can be used.

Since the Z88 does not come with a hard disk (not even a floppy disk), there seems little point in using this system, and it has not been noted in this book.

A few other filing commands may be used in your everyday use of the machine, however. For all these commands you can *preselect* up to two files by placing the cursor over the file name when FILER runs, and pressing ENTER (for the first file) and then SHIFT ENTER (for the second). These preselections avoid the need to type filenames in other commands.

1 The ◇ CF command allows you to catalogue your files. You can specify a filename, or press ENTER to list all files. For each file you will see the date and time of the creation of the file and the date and time when the file was last amended. The file length, in number of characters, is also shown.

2 The ◇ CO command allows you to make a copy of a file. You are prompted for the filename of the source and of the destination. You can use names like :RM.0/myfil :RAM.1/myfil in this way to make a copy in the extended memory.

3 ◇ RE allows you to rename a file which must remain in the same part of the memory.

4 ◇ ER will erase a file, though not a file that is in use such as a directory.

5 The ◇ CE, ◇ ES and ◇ EF commands are specialised
commands for filing with EPROMS, the type of memory that
is not erased except by removing it from the machine and
treating with ultraviolet light.

Appendix A
Diamond Key Actions

This list of actions obtained by using the ◇ key does not include the actions of the cursor arrowed keys, only the letter keys. Several entries have been duplicated in order to make it easier to find actions that could be listed under different headings.

Action	Keys	Action	Keys
Add column	◇ EAC	Delete column	◇ EDC
Align to centre	◇ LAC	Delete file	◇ ER
Align to left	◇ LAL	Delete row	◇ Y
Align to right	◇ LAR	Delete row in column	◇ EDRC
Alternate font print	◇ PA	Delete suspended work	◇ KILL
Block highlight	◇ PHB	Delete to end of slot	◇ D
Block list/print	◇ BL	Delete word	◇ T
Block marker	◇ Z	Device for filing	◇ SV
Bold print	◇ PB	Diary memory free	◇ EMF
Bottom file in list	◇ FB	Edit expression	◇ X
Card display (RAM or EPROM)	◇ CARD	Enter new printer driver	◇ FU
Catalogue EPROM	◇ CE	EPROM fetch	◇ EF
Catalogue files	◇ CF	EPROM save	◇ ES
Centre align	◇ LAC	Erase file	◇ ER
Change case	◇ S	Execute file of commands	◇ EX
Change expression/text slot	◇ ENT	Expression/text slot change	◇ ENT
Clear block marking	◇ Q	Extended sequence print	◇ PX
Copy block	◇ BC	File catalogue	◇ CF
Copy file	◇ CO	File copy	◇ CO
Count words	◇ BWC	File erase	◇ ER
Create directory	◇ CD	File load	◇ FL
Create expression slot	◇ X	File name	◇ FC
Decimal places in slot	◇ LDP	File rename	◇ RE
Default format	◇ LDF	File save	◇ FS
Delete Block	◇ BD		
Delete character	◇ G		

153

Diamond Key Actions

Action	Keys	Action	Keys
First active day in diary	◇ CFAD	Print special characters(s)	◇ PX
First column	◇ CFC	Purge system	◇ PURGE
Fix column	◇ LFC	Recalculate spreadsheet	◇ A
Fix row	◇ LFR	Reformat paragraph	◇ R
Format paragraph	◇ R	Release alignment	◇ LAF
Free align	◇ LAF	Rename file	◇ RE
Go to slot	◇ CGS	Remove highlights	◇ PHR
Highlight block	◇ PHB	Replace word/phrase	◇ BRP
Insert character	◇ U	Replicate slot(s)	◇ BRE
Insert column	◇ EIC	Reset default printer driver	◇ FNEW
Insert highlights	◇ PHI	Reset system	◇ PURGE
Insert page	◇ EIP	Restore cursor position	◇ CRP
Insert/Overtype change	◇ V	Right align	◇ LAR
Insert reference	◇ K	Right-hand margin	◇ H
Insert row	◇ N	Save cursor position	◇ CSP
Insert row in column	◇ EIRC	Save file	◇ FS
Italic print	◇ PI	Save to EPROM	◇ ES
Join lines	◇ EJL	Search for word/phrase	◇ BSE
Kill suspended activity	◇ KILL	Select another option	◇ J
Last active day in diary	◇ CLAD	Select device (filer)	◇ SV
Last file in list	◇ FB	Select directory	◇ SI
Leading characters(s)	◇ LCL	Set margin (right)	◇ H
Left align	◇ LAL	Sign brackets	◇ LSB
Left/centre/right align	◇ LLCR	Sign minus	◇ LSM
List block or print	◇ BL	Slot width	◇ W
Load from EPROM	◇ EF	Sort into order	◇ BSO
Load in file	◇ FL	Split line	◇ ESL
Mark block	◇ Z	Subscript print	◇ PL
Memory free (Diary)	◇ EMF	Superscript print	◇ PR
Microspace pitch	◇ PM	Swap case	◇ S
Minus as – sign	◇ LSM	Text/expression slot change	◇ ENT
Minus as ( ) sign	◇ LSB	Text margin	◇ H
Move block	◇ BM	Today in Diary	◇ CT
Move to first column	◇ CFC	Top file in list	◇ FT
Move to last column	◇ CLC	Trailing characters(s)	◇ LCT
Move to slot	◇ CGS	Tree copy (extended directory)	◇ TC
Name file	◇ FC	Underline	◇ PU
Name match (for directory)	◇ NM	User defined print	◇ PE
New text	◇ BNEW	Width of slot/tab position	◇ W
Next file in list	◇ FN	Word count	◇ BWC
Next find/replace	◇ BNM		
Next option	◇ J		
Options page	◇ O		
Previous file in list	◇ FP		
Previous find/replace	◇ BPM		
Print block	◇ BL		
Print document	◇ PO		

Appendix B
Commands in Alarm and CLI Files

When a command or set of commands has to be included into an Alarm setting, the commands have to be given in a different way, because pressing the ◇ or ☐ keys would have an immediate effect. The method that is used is to code these command keys, and·the same method is used for CLI files, meaning files in which commands can be included so that the machine can be made to go through a set of commands as the file is run.

The following are the substitutions that are used:

Normal character	Command character
#	☐
|	◇
##	#
~ ~	~
!!	!
SHIFT	~S
INDEX	~I
MENU	~M
HELP	~H
ENTER	~E
DEL	~X
TAB	~T
uparrow	~U
downarrow	~D
leftarrow	~L
rightarrow	~R
ESC	|[

Appendix C

Standard (Scientific) Form of Numbers

Standard form is a method of writing and working with numbers that are either very large or very small. The principle is that only a limited number of digits in a number are ever really significant. For example, if a poll calls for 10 000 people to be questioned, it does not really matter very much if the number happens to be 9990 or 10 010. Taking another example, a number like 0.000 000 126 842 314 might just as well be written as 0.000 000 127 unless there is some special need to use more than three significant figures.

To see why standard form is used, consider the number 1 000 000. If you wanted to multiply this by 1.5 you would not, I hope, go through the stages of saying: 'one point five times zero is zero, one point five times zero is zero . . .' for six times before coming to 'one point five times one is one point five'. You would, of course, simply say: 'one point five times a million is one point five million'. This is what standard form is all about. Each number, when put into standard form, consists of two parts. One part is a number that is between 1 and 10, and which will use as many significant figures as needed. If you settled for three figures following the decimal point, for example, you might use numbers like 1.776, 5.204, 9,917 and so on. The second part of each number is a power of ten. This is just a way of writing the zeros of the number, and showing whether it is greater than or less than unity. The multiplier 10 would be written as El, (one zero), 100 as E2 (two zeros) 1000 as E3 (three zeros) and so on. Fractions are written with a negative sign and a number that is one more than the number of zeros. This the multiplier 0.01 is written as E − 2, 0.001 as E − 3 and so on. Looking at an example, a complete number in standard form might be written as 1.617E3. This is the standard form of the number 1617. Similarly the number 4.116E − 3 is the standard form of the number 0.00116.

To put a number into standard form.

(1) Shift the decimal point until the number lies between 1 and 10. Count the number of decimal places, and note if the shift is left or right.

(2) Write the number that you now have, and chop off, or round off, all digits beyond the limit that you have decided on.

(3) Write down the E, and if you have had to shift the decimal point right, add a negative sign.

(4) Follow this with the number of places that you had to shift the decimal point.

Examples

    (a) 1 814 519 371 402

The number of figures to be used is 5. Shift the point 12 places left, and write down five figures, getting 1.8145. Since the point was shifted 12 places, the number is 1.8145E12

    (b) 0.000 000 000 141 536

The number of places to be used is 4. Shift the point ten places right and chop to four figures, getting 1.415. Because the shift was of ten places right, the multiplier is E − 10, so that the number in standard form is 1.415E − 10.

Converting back from standard form.

(1) If the sign that follows the E is negative, then the point is moved left, else move the point right.

(2) Move the point, filling out with zeros where there are no digits to use.

Examples:

    (a) 3.124E8

Move eight places right to get 312 400 000 − the five zeros are used to fill in spaces.

    (b) 4.198E − 4

Move four places left, inserting zeros to get .0 004 198.

Appendix D
Device Filenames

The filename convention of the Z88 allows for a main name of up to twelve characters, to which can be added a three-character extension. This follows the convention set by other machines, except that most other machines in common use allow only eight-character filenames. To preserve compatibility, it is therefore preferable to keep to a maximum of eight characters for names.

The Z88 also allows a *designator* which corresponds to the drive letter A:, B;, C; etc., used by PC and other machines. The form used by the Z88, however, is more elaborate and allows blocks of memory and other destinations or sources of files to be specified. The form of the designator is colon–name–dot–digit–slash, following which is the filename (which can include a directory reference). The list of device designators is:

Code form	Device
:RAM.0	internal memory
:RAM.1	Added RAM, card 1
:RAM.2	Added RAM, card 2
:RAM.3	Added RAM, card 3
:RAM. –	RAM used temporarily
:SCR.0	Screen
:PRT.0	Printer
:NUL.0	Null
:COM.0	Serial input/output

Note: the uses of these last four device names are very limited. The :COM.0 designator can be used for reading in files from another machine (see Part 9), but not necessarily for sending out data. You can, however, use the :COM.0 designator in the destination file-name of a Copy command to copy a file to a serial printer. The :PRT.0 designator has no effect on a serial printer. The :NUL.0 designator is intended to allow a file to be sent nowhere – a method of checking what happens when a file copy command is used. Use of these designators with PipeDream files causes either the *File type mismatch* or the *File not found* error message.

The <> SV command of Filer can be used to designate a default device to replace the :RAM.0 which is the normal default RAM. Once again, this should not be used with the last four designators apart from :COM.0.

Index